THE PICTORIAL HISTORY OF
TENNIS

THE PICTORIAL HISTORY OF
TENNIS
SEAN CALLERY

GALLERY BOOKS
An imprint of W.H. Smith Publishers Inc.
112 Madison Avenue
New York, New York 10016

Contents

Published by Gallery Books
A Division of W H Smith Publishers Inc.
112 Madison Avenue
New York, New York 10016

Produced by
Brompton Books Corp.
15 Sherwood Place
Greenwich, CT 06830

ISBN 0-8317-6916-5

Printed in Hong Kong

10 9 8 7 6 5 4 3 2 1

PAGE 1: *John McEnroe at the US
Open.*

PAGES 2-3: *A capacity-crowd at
Flushing Meadow.*

OVERLEAF: *The legendary Bjorn
Borg.*

INTRODUCTION

Tennis is a beautiful game. It is a battle which blends guile with aggression, technique with artistry, speed of thought with flowing movement, mental with physical effort. It is also one of the great participant and spectator sports of the twentieth century: it has been estimated that more than 127 million people in the world play tennis. Most of them are fans, too. They know that for drama and excitement few sights can rival that moment when server and receiver's eyes meet across the net, and the ball is launched for the first strike to commence a key point.

Developed from ancient ball and racket games, and taken up by the Victorian gentry in Britain, tennis really took off after the First World War. That period has been called the 'Golden Age' of tennis, when the game's stars achieved equal rank with the stars of the silver screen. Tennis was glamorous, and, the sport spread across the world. Those who ran it opened, then eventually closed, a divide between professional and amateur players that reeked of hypocrisy and cheated the public.

The game today is an international carousel, offering huge rewards and imposing a punishing mental and physical strain. Truly global, the game transcends frontiers in a way that few modern sports do – you can talk tennis anywhere in the world.

The rewards offered to a small band of today's top players are extremely high: teen-agers can become millionaires. One tournament even dangles a diamond encrusted racket in front of their eyes as an inducement! The power of business is illustrated by the fact that less than half the top ten players use the racket of their choice: endorsements, not prize money, are a route to lifelong financial security for those so much in the public eye.

Tennis is fortunate in that its format is compatible with the demands of television. An oblong court, easy access to views of anguished faces, and regular breaks in play (allowing for commercials), have proved an ideal formula for the TV coverage which has done so much to promote the game.

But forget the internal political struggles, the game has a strength of its own. The rules have hardly changed in more than 100 years, and tennis retains a beautiful simplicity of form, which produces a marvelous spectacle. This book celebrates that beauty, and re-joices in the fascinating history of a tremendous game, in which colorful personalities and controversial incidents abound.

PART I
Origins and Development until 1914

ABOVE: *Sir John Lavery's* The
Tennis Party *captures the spirit of
Victorian tennis: an opportunity for
the young to flirt under the watchful
eyes of their elders.*

The Hourglass Game

LEFT: *Real tennis could be played in a variety of settings, provided they were walled in.*

BELOW: *Even in the 18th century, the French experimented with racket designs.*

The story of tennis spans much of man's history – the ancient Egyptians, the Roman Empire, the monasteries of medieval France – but the catalyst was the need in English Victorian society for a game where young people could meet decorously at garden parties.

Games in which a ball is struck, either with the hand or an implement, date back thousands of years. In 2000 BC the Egyptians played ball, in 425 BC Homer described a ball game in the Odyssey, and similar sporting activities were popular for a time during the Roman Empire. By the twelfth century, 'Royal Tennis,' or 'Real' or 'Court Tennis' as it has also been called, was being played in the cloisters of French monasteries. Known as *Jeu de Paume* (the 'game of the palm') it involved hitting a ball with the hand, and later, with a racket, in a confined space where walls, windows, pillars, and roofs were all part of the court. Royalty enjoyed the complex game: Henry VIII of England and Henry II of France were both said to be excellent players, and the English king had his own court built at Hampton Court Palace.

By the nineteenth century an outdoor version of the game, called 'long tennis', was in existence. In 1858 solicitor Major Harry Gem marked out a court on the croquet lawn belonging to his Spanish friend Augurio Perera, and in 1872 the major formed the world's first tennis club at Leamington Spa in the English Midlands.

In late 1873, an eccentric puzzle games inventor, Major Walter Clopton Wingfield launched a version of tennis which he called 'Sphairistike'. (The name was the Greek for 'ball game', but was quickly abbreviated to 'Sticky'.) Wingfield stipulated that the court should be a distorted figure of eight, like an hourglass, with a five foot-high net (borrowed from the game of badminton) dividing the two sides. It contained uncovered rubber balls imported from Germany – the sort used for Eton fives. The game attracted much publicity, stimulating interest in playing tennis, although many people declined to buy the major's kit, and simply strung a net up across their croquet lawns, creating their own variations of a game by now popularly known as lawn tennis.

The beauty of the game for Victorian society was that many middle class homes had croquet lawns, but interest in croquet itself was declining. Young people wanted a more energetic, outdoor game where they could flirt with the opposite sex without alarming their parents. The thrills, spills and excitement of tennis on the lawn under watchful parental eyes was the perfect solution.

This middle class influence on the game has been strong in just about every country where tennis is played. Tennis became a social game for the well-off, and tennis clubs have traditionally been the preserve of the more privileged. Tennis history has various examples of great players who came through because of this background (Helen Wills, Bill Tilden) and some who became champions despite their humble origins (Billie Jean King, Fred Perry).

The All England Croquet Club in Worple Road, Wimbledon took an interest in the game, and set some land aside for a tennis court, completed in 1875. It also took over the rules of the game from the Marylebone Cricket Club (the MCC), which also controled rackets and real tennis. A dynamic trio of Henry Jones, Julian Marshall and C G Heathcote decided on some major rule changes in 1875, which have remained the basis of the game ever since.

The court became rectangular, 78 feet long by 27 feet wide. The rackets scoring system recommended by Wingfield (in which only the server could increase his score) was dropped, replaced by the 15,30,40, deuce and advantage scoring of real tennis. Servers should have two chances to commence each point, and the net height was reduced in 1882 to 3 feet 6 inches at the posts.

These rules were used for the first of the Wimbledon tennis tour-

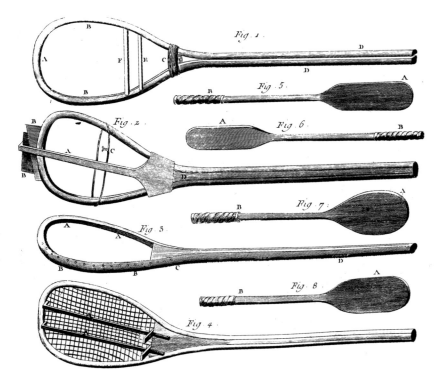

THE HIGH BORNE PRINCE IAMES DVKE OF YORKE
borne October - the 13 1633

ABOVE: *James, Duke of York, apparently a devotee of 'royal tennis' at an early age.*

naments in 1877 and the Lawn Tennis Association, formed in 1888, took over legislative control from the All England Croquet and Lawn Tennis Club. It was not the first tennis association, that honor going to the New Orleans Lawn Tennis Club formed in 1876.

At this stage it is worth examining how different elements of the game came about. First, the word 'tennis' probably evolved from the French verb *tenir*, meaning 'take', or as we would say, 'play!' before each point. Another possibility is that early versions of the game had five players on each side, earning the name 'tens'. The service prob-

ably originated in the real tennis habit of having the ball simply thrown into play by an outside party – usually a servant.

The scoring also harks back to real tennis, where a clock was used to keep the score, the hands being moved a quarter of the way around the face for each point. 'Love', as the word for no score, has two possible beginnings: it could be from the French for egg, *l'oeuf*, which is shaped like a nought, or could be an echo of how the word 'love' can be used to mean 'nothing' as in 'All for Love'. 'Deuce' comes from the French phrase *deux a jouer* for two points to play.

The new game spread quickly through Europe, rapidly becoming almost as popular in France as it was in Britain, particularly in the south, where wealthy families took to entertaining with tennis parties. Some Englishmen on holiday formed a club at Dinard in 1878, and the first national championships were held at the Ile de Plateaux, Paris, in 1891. Although officially restricted to those of French birth, the first champion was in fact English. Women were admitted to the championships in 1897.

It was members of a British colony in Bordeghera who formed the first Italian tennis club in 1878, but the Italians took to the game enthusiastically and by 1898 there were 700 courts in the land, only a few of them grass. Championships began in 1894, but folded four years later, and real expansion resumed when the Italian Tennis Federation was formed in 1910.

The first National Championships for men in Germany were inaugurated in 1892, the women following four years later. In 1902 the *Deutscher Lawn Tennis Bund* was founded, 24 years after the first courts had been laid by British enthusiasts. For many years tennis in Germany was very much an aristocrat's pastime.

Czechoslovakia ranks alongside Britain and France in the early history of tennis: real tennis was played in Bohemia during the fifteenth and sixteenth centuries at the height of European interest in the game. The new form of tennis grew rapidly from the 1880s, fueled by an 1879 competition at Chocen that offered cash prizes.

By the early years of the twentieth century, the game had followers throughout Europe. The second major tennis tournament in the world was held in Ireland in 1879 and was the first championship to hold a women's singles and mixed doubles competition. In Rumania the first clubs were formed in 1898, and the first national championships were held in 1911. The Swedish Crown Prince, later King Gustav V, returned from England a keen tennis fan in 1879, and became a frequent competitor in tournaments. And tennis was introduced to Russia in 1890; a notable winner of the women's singles

TOP: *Lucas van Gassel's* King David giving Uriah his letter to Joab *shows a number of 16th century courtly pursuits, among them, tennis. Note the use of a rope rather than a net to divide the court.*

ABOVE: *The tree inconveniently close to the court, as well as the bulky bonnet illustrate that practical and functional were not prime requirements in Victorian tennis.*

RIGHT: *Acceptable tennis apparel for men was a good deal more practical than women's garb.*

at the 1914 Russian Championships in St Petersburg was the American Elizabeth Ryan.

Various parts of the British Empire took up the game too. The first Australian International Championships were held in 1905 in Melbourne, although informal tournaments had taken place since the 1880s. The first national champion was Rodney Heath, and two years later the title holder, Norman Brookes, traveled to England to become the first overseas player to lift the men's singles trophy at Wimbledon.

In India, the Punjab Championships at the Lahore Gymkana in 1885 commenced five years after the British introduced tennis to the sub-continent. The game slowly grew in popularity and in 1920, the All India Lawn Tennis Association was formed. The strong British influence in South Africa ensured a rapid growth of the game, and the first South African championship was held in 1891.

The inauguration of the Davis Cup in 1900 was a further spur to the development of international tennis, and by 1913 an international regulatory body was required. Twelve countries were represented at the inaugural meeting of the International Lawn Tennis Federation (ILTF), and America affiliated ten years later. Tennis was on its way to becoming a major sport across the world.

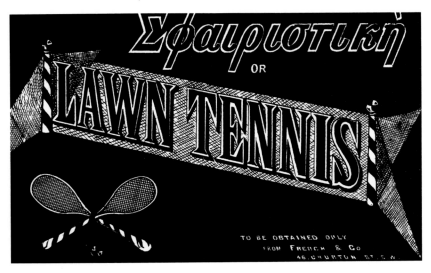

AN ILLUSTRATED WEEKLY NEWSPAPER

No. 719.—Vol. XXVIII.
Reg⁴. at General Post Office as a Newspaper]
SATURDAY, SEPTEMBER 8, 1883
WITH EXTRA SUPPLEMENT [
PRICE SIXPENCE
Or by Post Sixpence Halfpeny

FAR LEFT: *The rule book for one of Wingfield's sphairistike kits.*

TOP LEFT: *Puzzles inventor, and popularizer of tennis, Major Walton Clopton Wingfield.*

BOTTOM LEFT: *By 1892 lawn tennis was the height of fashion. But everything stopped for tea.*

ABOVE: *The 1888 Wimbledon championship match – the year Ernest Renshaw kept up the family tradition and won the title.*

LEFT: *The royal connection continues as the Prince of Wales plays tennis at a new club in Baden-Baden, Germany.*

The Birth of Wimbledon

The Lawn Tennis Championships held at Wimbledon began when the All England Croquet and Lawn Tennis Club, short of cash and needing to repair a pony roller, decided to hold a fund raising tournament. The Championships have since become the tournament every tennis player in the world wants to win, and the roller is still on Centre Court. It is too wide to go through any of the exits.

The tournament was announced on 9 June 1877 in *The Field*, which had donated a 25 guinea cup as first prize. The 22 gentlemen who entered were charged one guinea for the privilege, and play began at 3.30pm on Monday 9 July. The final was delayed first by rain and then put back to avoid clashing with the Eton vs Harrow cricket match at Lords, which was considered a much greater attraction.

The first Wimbledon title was won by Spencer Gore, a 27-year-old surveyor. A real tennis and rackets enthusiast, he had a fine understanding of tactics and appreciated the new ruling that the net should be 5 feet high at the posts and 3 feet 3 inches in the middle, forcing most shots to be played over the center of the net. So, playing William Marshall, a Cambridge tennis blue, he attacked the net whenever he could, angling volleys to the sides of the court. In his enthusiasm he seems to have struck some of these volleys while the ball was still in his opponent's court, and in 1880 a rule was introduced banning striking the ball before it crossed the net.

It is one of the ironies of the game that its first champion was highly dismissive about the future of tennis. Gore felt it lacked variety and interest compared with, say, cricket or rackets, and that this would 'prevent lawn tennis in its present form from taking rank among our great games.'

The next year Gore had the luxury of watching 34 entrants compete for the right to play him in the Challenge Round for the title – the system of the preceding year's winner facing only one opponent for the championship was retained until 1922. He lost to Frank

ABOVE: *Twins William and Ernest Renshaw dominated Wimbledon for a decade.*

RIGHT: *Maud Watson, the first women's champion, receives a Jubilee Medal from Queen Mary at the 1927 celebrations.*

ABOVE RIGHT: *A familiar sight to Wimbledon spectators: pulling on the covers.*

FAR RIGHT: *New Zealander Anthony Wilding who was later to win three Wimbledon singles titles.*

Hadow, who was on leave from a coffee plantation in Ceylon. Hadow introduced a new tennis stroke, repeatedly lobbing the ball over the tall Gore, who was left stranded at the net.

Hadow was unable to return for the 1879 tournament, which was distinguished for two reasons. One finalist, clergyman John Hartley, did not expect to get very far in the tournament and had to rush back to his Yorkshire parish in the north of England to undertake his Sunday duties, and then travel back by train the following morning in time to play. Tired and hungry, he lost the first set, but was rescued by a break for rain, and returned refreshed to clinch the match 2-6, 6-0, 6-1, 6-1. The man he beat in the final was the only Wimbledon finalist (so far) to be convicted later for murder. (Vere Thomas St Leger Goold, playing under the pseudonym St Leger, was the younger son of an Irish baronet. In 1907 he murdered a Danish widow in the south of France, and attempted to send her dismembered body to England in two trunks. Caught and convicted, he ended his days on Devil's Island.)

The following quarter century at Wimbledon was dominated by the Renshaw twins William and Ernest, and the Doherty brothers Reggie and Laurie.

The Renshaws inherited sufficient money when their father died to be able to pursue tennis as much more than an idle pastime. William Renshaw was the better player, stronger and cooler, and he was the first player at Wimbledon to be seen to hit the ball while it was at its highest point in midair: the 'Renshaw smash' became a famous stroke. He won the Challenge Round seven times between 1881 and 1889 and in 1888 Ernest Renshaw took the title. The identical twins were a formidable – and no doubt confusing – doubles team, winning five titles in six years after the doubles game was in-

troduced at Wimbledon in 1884. The Renshaws became popular public figures and helped to raise the profile of the game – in 1885 3500 spectators were attracted to watch William in the final round. Their aggressive style of play made them virtually invincible, and entry rates for the tournament dropped for a while as other players decided not to be humiliated by a Renshaw.

Two more identical twins, Herbert and Wilfred Baddeley from Kent, took over the Renshaw mantle in the next decade, winning five doubles and three singles titles in eight years. Wilfred's singles win in 1891 at the age of 19 years, 5 months and 23 days made him the youngest men's singles title holder until Boris Becker in 1985.

Amazingly, the next great names in Wimbledon history were also brothers (but not twins); Reggie and Laurie Doherty were born in

Wimbledon itself and played spectacular and stylish tennis that was well above the standard of anything seen before. In the ten years from 1897 Reggie won four singles finals, Laurie five, and in the doubles they took the title eight times. Renowned for their sportsmanship, the Doherty brothers did much to establish the popularity of tennis, and were idolized by the fans.

Although Wimbledon began as very much a British event, the tournament gradually attracted players from around the world, and in 1905 the 71 entries in the men's contest included three Australasians, four Americans, and players from Belgium, Denmark, Sweden and South Africa. Two years later the men's title left Britain for the first time, when the slender but tough Australian Norman Brookes won by default because Laurie Doherty was not well enough to play.

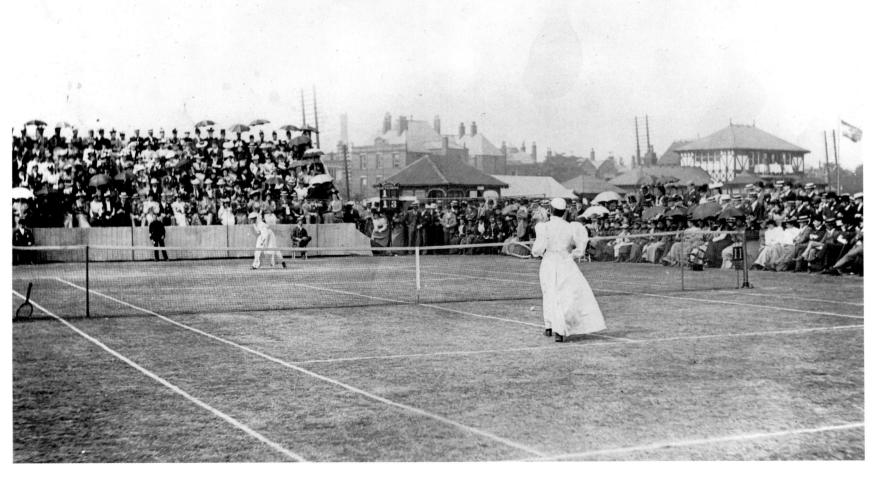

The title went to an antipodean again in 1910 when Anthony Wilding of New Zealand won the first of three successive finals. Wilding was a Cambridge undergraduate who took a highly professional attitude to his tennis, persuading the authorities to let him practise in the city's Corn Exchange which housed a vegetable market most of the time.

The women's tournament at Wimbledon was started as a last minute decision in 1884, and won by Maud Watson. The championship went on to be dominated for years by a young woman who aroused great affection in the crowd and did much to establish women's tennis as a credible sport.

Lottie Dod was born in Cheshire in 1871 and modeled her game on the attacking Renshaw brothers. A tall tomboy, Lottie possessed a fine forehand drive and loved to volley and smash, although she served underarm. She was the youngest-ever title winner at 15 years 9 months; she never lost at Wimbledon and only ever dropped one set there – although women's tennis was not as competitive as the men's game at this time. Perhaps because of this, she retired from the game aged 21, became captain of the English hockey team and then took up golf, winning the 1904 British Ladies' Golf Championship.

The next British woman to have a major impact on Wimbledon began to attract attention at the age Lottie Dod left the game. Dorothea Lambert Chambers (née Douglass) was, in tennis terms, a late developer, reaching her first Wimbledon championship in 1902 aged 23, and losing her first final the next year. She was to win seven singles titles in all, and usually gave her opponents a sound drubbing – notably the 6-0, 6-0 trouncing of Dora Boothby in 1911.

An outstanding athlete, Dorothea Lambert Chambers was a badminton doubles champion and an excellent hockey player. Four of her title wins were achieved by playing through to the Challenge Round. Whether battling through to meet the title holder was an advantage, as it tightened up the game, or a drawback because of the extra effort required while the champion relaxed and waited, is still debatable.

The woman she lost to in the 1905 final, May Sutton, caused a stir by playing at Wimbledon with her sleeves rolled up. More significantly, she was the first player to take a Wimbledon title overseas to America. A happy, charming character, May Sutton hit her forehand drives with unheard of power, and won two singles titles in three consecutive finals, all of them against Dorothea Chambers.

By the time the First World War stopped Wimbledon's annual championships, there had been 31 women's championships, with ten women having won the title, only one of them not British. As tennis spread across the world and more women began to play, the British dominance was to end. The Wimbledon championships had not only become part of the sporting scene, they also played a role in British social life as magazines started to carry articles advising ladies on what to wear to Wimbledon. After 38 meetings, its future, interrupted as it must be, was assured.

ABOVE: *Dorothea Lambert Chambers who learned to play tennis just by hitting a ball against a wall.*

BELOW: *Scenes from some of the championship matches of 1887, lampooned by a contemporary cartoonist.*

ABOVE, FAR LEFT: *All-rounder Lottie Dod during the 1890s.*

ABOVE LEFT: *America's May Sutton caused raised eyebrows by daring to roll up her sleeves.*

LEFT: *Lottie Dod in action at Wimbledon, 1897.*

Tennis goes West

ABOVE: *Tennis in Prospect Place,*
New York, 1885, 11 years after the
game reached America.

Tennis reached America very soon after it began gaining popularity in England. In early 1874 Mary Ewing Outerbridge returned to the family home in Staten Island from a holiday in Bermuda, where she had seen the game played, bringing with her the first tennis set to reach the US. It was set up by her brother on the turf of the Staten Island Cricket and Baseball Club.

A year later, Dr James Dwight graduated from Harvard and went on a trip to Europe. He returned with a Sphairistike set, and a court was set up at the house of his uncle William Appleton, in Nahant, Massachusetts. Dwight was closely involved in the development of the game in America from then on. He was to be chief executive of the United States Lawn Tennis Association for 21 years, and in 1884 was the first American to play at Wimbledon.

Tennis was predominantly the preserve of the East Coast between Boston and Staten Island, but down in the south, British visitors brought Sphairistike kits with them, leading to the formation of the New Orleans Lawn Tennis Club in 1876, the first of its kind in the United States. In 1876 Dwight won the first tournament to be held in the country – a round robin handicap* in Nahant, Massachusetts – beating F R Sears Jr 12-15, 15-7, 15-13 (using the rackets scoring system). Over the next few years the game was incubated in the Boston and New England area, where famous names such as Dwight, Richard Sears, Dwight Davis and Hazel Hotchkiss Wightman were all to play a part in the growth of tennis.

In September 1880 an Englishman, O E Woodhouse, who had reached the Wimbledon all-comers final two months previously,

happened to be in America, and won the first unofficial American Championships in a field of 33, at the Staten Island Cricket and Baseball Club.

At this time every club made its own rules on net height, scoring, ball dimensions, and so on. Dr Dwight and F R Sears refused to play in protest at the balls being used, and Dwight joined with other tennis figures, including Emilius Outerbridge (brother of Mary Outerbridge), to push for the establishment of a National Association to standardize rules and regulate the game. On 21 May 1881, representatives of 34 tennis clubs met at the Fifth Avenue Hotel in New York City to form the United States Lawn Tennis Association (USLTA). Since Outerbridge and Dwight were rivals for the leadership, a compromise president, General R S Oliver, was elected. Over the next few years the Association stipulated a court length of 78 feet, a net 3 feet high at the center, a uniform ball, and emphasized that the umpire's decision was final – an early indication, perhaps of undesirable on-court behaviour.

In 1881, the Association organized the inaugural official US Championship at the Newport Casino, played on grass, entry open to all. Nineteen-year-old Richard Sears of Boston (younger brother of F R Sears) won in a field of 25 men. He was to hold the title for seven years running, and win the doubles for six consecutive years. Both these records still stand.

The USLTA first allowed foreign players to compete in the championships in 1884. The previous year American players had visited

*A 'round robin' tournament was one in which each player played everyone else.

Hovey beat the first family team to compete in the nationals, Carr Baker Neel and Samuel R Neel.

Women's tennis was growing apace, too. 1892 had seen the first triple crown, won by Irish-born Mabel Cahill, the first non-American champion. She retained her singles and doubles titles from the previous year, and won the mixed as well, partnered by C Hobart. Three years later the first of three singles titles was won by one of the pioneers of American tennis, Juliette Atkinson of Brooklyn. She appeared in the Challenge Round every year from 1895 to 1899, winning in 1895, 1897 and 1898. She also won the doubles title seven times and the mixed three times. Her feats were matched in the men's tournament by a powerful left hander and all-round athlete called Robert Wrenn, who won the singles title four times out of five between 1893 and 1897, the first at the age of 19.

Wrenn's successor as the top men's player was Bill Larned, a tough, stocky graduate from Cornell University who played an aggressive, fast game and possessed a lethal backhand. Larned won his first championship aged 28 in 1901, and retained it the next year with a win over Britain's Reggie Doherty. The Briton's brother Laurie avenged the defeat the next year, but Larned was champion again in 1907 and won it for the last time in 1911, at the age of 38 – the oldest men's title holder ever. Laurie Doherty's 1903 win over Larned, 6-0, 6-3, 10-8, was the first time the title had gone abroad, and he teamed up with his brother that year to retain the doubles title too.

After a tour of the West Coast in 1899, tennis had taken a firm hold in California, where superb players were produced who established the tennis dominance of the Pacific Coast. May Sutton was one such pioneer. Living in Pasadena, California but born in Plymouth, England, she was the youngest player to win the US women's singles in 1904 at 16 years 9 months (a record since beaten by Tracy Austin). She went on to win two Wimbledon titles and was still playing in 1925 when she reached the US doubles finals.

Another Californian woman who had a major impact on tennis was Hazel Hotchkiss, who married to become Hazel Wightman. (The story of how she founded the Wightman Cup is told later.) Born in Healdsburg, she won the US singles four times between 1909 and 1919, and the doubles and mixed six times each. She arrived in style in 1909 by winning the triple crown. It was a year when the West Coast men caused a stir, too, for Maurice McLoughlin and Thomas Bundy reached the final and semi-final respectively playing fast, sharp tennis learned on hard courts and perfected on grass

England, playing such luminaries as the Renshaw brothers, and had returned with spiked shoes that were more suitable for games on grass. The Challenge Round system, where the title holder plays only one match against the player who won through the tournament, was introduced in 1884. The format was used in the States until 1912.

By 1885, the game was growing fast and the USLTA authorized a number of sectional championships, and switched to the deuce/advantage scoring system. These regional championships were evidence of the spread of the game to the west, leading to the commencement of the Western Championships in Chicago in 1887. The game was becoming popular with women too, and in the same year the first women's singles tournament was staged at the Philadelphia Cricket Club. In 1890, the men's singles draw attracted 53 entrants for the US Championship, and for the first time the doubles format matched eastern and western sectional winners in a final, the winners playing the title holders. Tennis was getting more public support and the next year large crowds were gathering every morning at the Casino for the nine days of the championship.

Three years later, for the only time in the history of the national championships, an event was held off the Eastern Seaboard. Chicago was staging the World Fair, and the doubles championship, held at St George's Cricket Club, was won by Clarence Hobart and Fred Hovey on 24 July. Back at Newport the next year, Hobart and

ABOVE: *Sphairistike sets were the key to the tennis invasion of America.*

RIGHT: *Holcombe Ward and Dwight Davis in 1901.*

ABOVE: *Reggie and Laurie Doherty, 1908. In 1903 Laurie became the first foreign winner of the US Championship, also winning the doubles with his brother the same year.*

LEFT: *May Sutton, for many years the youngest women's champion.*

ABOVE LEFT: *Americans May Sutton and Elizabeth Ryan in 1908 at Wimbledon.*

ABOVE FAR RIGHT *Hazel Wightman and Miss Zinderston at the 1919 championships.*

RIGHT: *Norwegian-born US champion Molla Mallory in an aggressive pose.*

during a tour from Minneapolis to Brooklyn prior to the championships. Their play helped to popularize tennis because it was physically demanding, and exciting to watch. McLoughlin, who became known as 'Red Mac', and 'The Californian Comet', later caused a sensation in the 1914 Davis Cup matches against Australia by beating the brilliant Norman Brookes in three sets.

In 1911 the Challenge Round was played for the last time. Larned clinched his seventh title, and the championships changed format to force the title holder to play through to the final in future. The following year, one of the great names of tennis, Bill Tilden, won his first title – the mixed – partnered by a top woman player who had spotted his potential, Mary K Browne. She also won the singles that year, and kept the title for two more years. Born in Santa Monica, California, Mary K Browne had a lethal forehand drive and excellent command of the game, and was the third top woman player to emerge from California.

The 34th men's championship was held at Newport in 1914 for the last time, switching the next year to the West Side Tennis Club, Forest Hills. The wisdom of the decision was illustrated by the 5000-strong crowds who attended – over 1000 more people than the Newport Casino championship court could accommodate.

Over in Philadelphia at the women's tournament, Molla Bjurstedt (later Molla Mallory) was winning the first of eight singles titles. Born in Norway, Molla Mallory was the greatest American player prior to Helen Wills, and played with gritty endurance and a mighty forehand drive, compensating for a weak serve and backhand. Norwegian champion for ten years, she went to America in 1914, and was quickly established in the top ranks. Her 1916 singles win was achieved in an insultingly fast 22 minutes, dropping only one game against Louise Hammond Raymond.

The most significant aspect of those 1916 championships (apart from the fact that most of the other tennis playing nations were at war), was the commencement of the national boys and junior championships. The popularity of tennis in the USA at this time is reinforced by the existence of national indoor championships (begun in 1898) and clay court championships (in 1910). This new junior championship was part of a program of tennis development by the USLTA for men's and women's games and led to American domination of world tennis in the 1920s and 1930s.

An Idealist's Vision

The Davis Cup has become a major global men's tennis competition, in which national teams battle for the honor of winning, setting aside the individual gains that usually dominate so much in tennis. It was begun in 1900 when, in an act of extraordinary foresight and philanthropism, Dwight Filley Davis presented a silver bowl to the United States Lawn Tennis Association, for other countries to challenge and play for.

Davis was from St Louis, Missouri, but he learned tennis while on holiday at Magnolia, Massachusetts. The game was most popular on the East Coast, and when he took part in the first tennis tour in America in 1899, Davis was inspired by the interest the game generated on the West Coast. If it could make such an impact within one country, the benefits of this enthusiasm shared between countries could be boundless, he reasoned. He sounded out the father of American lawn tennis, Dr James Dwight, about the possibility of setting up an international competition, and the response encouraged 20-year-old Davis to order a 217-ounce silver punchbowl lined with gold from Boston silversmiths Shreve, Crump and Low.

The trophy cost $1000, and stood 13 inches (32.5cm) high, with a diameter of 18.5 inches (45cm) at its widest point. Etched on the interior rim were the words 'International Lawn Tennis Challenge Trophy. Presented by Dwight F. Davis, 1900'.

LEFT: *Dwight Davis, whose foresight and generosity began one of the most famous international contests.*

ABOVE: *James Dwight, the father of American tennis.*

James Dwight wrote to the British LTA early in 1900 inviting the British to challenge for the Cup in a bid to increase interest in lawn tennis. 'It might do a great deal for the game here, and possibly even with you it might be a help', he suggested. The LTA welcomed the idea, and it was agreed that the contest should consist of four singles and one doubles match. President of the British LTA, W H Collins suggested that the championship would be open to any nation with a recognized lawn tennis organization, although in 1900 only the British challenged.

A confident British team of Arthur Wentworth Gore, Edmund D Black and Herbert Roper Barrett (a solicitor who could only find

time to practise tennis on summer evenings, and who later served as a captain to several British Davis Cup teams) arrived in August for the contest against the Americans Holcombe Ward, Malcolm Whitman and Dwight Davis himself. The British were expecting an easy ride in Boston. They were wrong.

American tennis balls were slightly larger and softer than those used in Britain, and enabled the US players to open points with a fiendish 'twist' (kick) service, to which the British were completely unaccustomed. 'Not only did the ball screw, but it rose about 4 feet high in the shape of an egg', lamented *The Sportsman*. The British may also have been disturbed by the American practice of playing both singles games simultaneously on adjoining courts, forcing each player to cope not only with his own game, but to hear how his team mate was faring next door. Other factors such as the mere two days preparation the British allowed themselves after a sightseeing trip, and above all the considerable skill of the American players, contributed to a shock victory for the USA. The British vowed revenge.

They waited until 1902 to make their challenge, because the British wanted to use their two best players, the Doherty brothers

LEFT: *Arthur Wentworth Gore, a member of the first British Davis Cup team.*

BELOW LEFT: *The British waited until the Doherty brothers were free before making a second challenge for the Davis Cup in 1902.*

BELOW RIGHT: *Norman Brookes, a dynamic force in the first victorious Australian Davis Cup team in 1907.*

Laurie and Reggie. Thousands packed into the Crescent Athletic Club in New York that August to see the Americans win again. The next year the British at last won the cup, in dramatic circumstances. On the final day, with the rubber all square and his match in the fifth set, Laurie Doherty was 15-40 down on his own service with the score at four all. His opponent William Larned hit a winner off the first service to gain a vital break. But a linesman had deserted his post to catch a boat – and no one had noticed him leaving! The point was replayed, and Laurie survived to win the tie, and with it the Davis Cup for Britain.

With Britain as holder, Davis Cup matches transferred to the UK,

LEFT: *J C Parkes reaches for a smash against Maurice McLoughlin in 1913.*

ABOVE: *1913 South African Davis Cup team. (L-R) V R Gauntlett (captain), R F L Sueur, L E N Gindlestone and C R Leach.*

encouraging other European nations to compete, and forcing the USA to finance a long trip to challenge for the cup. Britain held on to the Davis Cup for three years, beating Belgium once, and the USA twice, mainly thanks to the famous Dohertys. In 1907, however, the tennis world was shocked by a new force in the game when the Australians captured the cup and retained it until 1911 as the pairing of Norman Brookes and Anthony Wilding held off all challenges. Tennis techniques were developing too. Brookes in particular learned to attack the American twist serve early as it rose and before it had slid too far away.

The Americans defeated Britain twice and South Africa by default to win the right to challenge the Australians, and in 1908 the two countries produced a classic Davis Cup tie when Wright defeated Brookes in the extreme heat of Melbourne. The American recovered from being two sets, 3-4 and 40-0 down, to win a thrilling match 12-10 in the final set. Wright's team mate Fred Alexander watched the battle enthralled from the court side – and promptly lost in straight sets to Wilding, who had spent the afternoon lying on a bed reading a book. Emotional strength has always been important in tennis!

For some European teams, a trip to Australia meant up to three months away from home and work, and few would even consider the journey. It was a struggle for the Americans too, and in 1912 they could not field a team for the Cup. There were suggestions that America should stop competing for the Davis Cup unless the Australians would bring it to the USA. In 1912, however, in another unexpected result, the British won the tie 3-2 and regained the trophy, and the return of the Davis Cup to Europe encouraged a record seven nations to contest it in the longest campaign yet. America emerged the victor for the first time since 1902.

The Davis Cup was established as a truly international tennis challenge. Although it did live up to its founder's ambition of uniting nations in friendly combat (and there are examples of sportsmanlike behaviour which cost nations a win), the patriotism of teams and crowds permeated the game too, adding a touch of jingoism to some of the contests. Indeed, from the ceremony of the draw (in which senior statesmen began to take part), to the custom of the umpires referring to the score by country, the nationalist element became increasingly central to the Davis Cup. Perhaps, given the circumstances in world politics at the time, this was inevitable.

PART II
International Growth
1919-1939

ABOVE: *Elizabeth Ryan (left) and Suzanne Lenglen in 1925 formed an intimidating doubles pairing.*

The Game Matures

LEFT: *Suzanne Lenglen and Bill Tilden, two of the most glamorous characters on the circuit.*

BELOW: *Advertisers seeking an image of style and glamour picked up on the appeal of tennis.*

RIGHT: *A notable photograph of Helen Wills and Helen Jacobs exchanging rare pleasantries.*

RIGHT: *Fred Perry was handsome, athletic and successful – but the British establishment loathed him.*

white racket that had never been seen before. As he left the court, a kite floated over the stadium, carrying the message: 'The white racket is a Slazenger'. Later, when it was feared he would turn professional, Slazenger sold him a house in Wimbledon for a nominal sum, then tried to get business associates to stump up the cash to buy it back for $100,000.

When players did opt for the professional tour, they were stripped of all their amateur club memberships, and hurled into a hectic, nomadic life of playing tennis anywhere the promoters could find a court. Gymnasiums, football stadiums, ice rinks, were among the venues where these stars played, usually on a canvas or wooden surface. A long match on canvas stretched over ice left their lower legs numb with cold.

Despite being regularly deprived of its latest champions, the amateur circuit continued to produce top quality tennis played at the best tennis venues in the world. For example in France, tennis

The years following the First World War were enriched with a glut of tennis talent. This period has been called the 'Golden Age' of tennis, because the game matured while retaining its sense of style, and produced great stars such as Suzanne Lenglen, Alice Marble, Helen Wills, the Four Musketeers, Fred Perry, Don Budge, and Bill Tilden. These players conducted a series of duels at tournaments around the world that captured the imagination of the media and pulled in the crowds. Would anyone take more than a solitary game from Lenglen? Which of the two Helens, Wills or Jacobs, would get the upper hand in their next battle? Which of the Four Musketeers would win the title – or would Bill Tilden hold them all off? It was a glamorous world and the top players were treated like Hollywood film idols – indeed, the two sets of stars often mixed together.

Yet there was a downside too. The game's elevated social origins were still apparent in the backgrounds of players such as Wills, Tilden, Lenglen and others. In this gentleman's game, the emergence of a professional circuit divided tennis even then. It was a poorly kept secret that the amateur players were receiving payments in one way or another. Suzanne Lenglen's father used to achieve this by insisting that he came as her manager, and that he be paid handsomely for this by the tournament. Sometimes a tennis official would place a golf ball six inches from the hole, and say to the tennis star: 'I bet you $100 that you can't hole that putt.' Many top players became full time employees of sports goods manufacturers, their only duty being to carry the right products on to the court.

Fred Perry's deal with Slazenger is one example. When he won the Australian championships in 1934, Perry was wielding a new, bright

was given a new home on the edge of the Bois de Boulogne near Paris, the Stade Roland Garros. The move was in response to France's sudden rise to dominate the tennis world in the early 1920s, challenging the mighty Americans, the persevering Britons, and the athletic Australians.

Tennis continued to build an international following, and much of the credit must go to the Davis Cup for creating interest in tennis as a team game between nations. For example, the Australian championships were not generally visited by players from other parts of the world (because of the length of the journey) unless they happened to be in the country for the Davis Cup. Australian tennis was active but a little isolated in the interwar years. From 1919 to 1940, the men's title was won by an Australian 17 times, notable exceptions being Jean Borotra in 1928, Fred Perry in 1934, and Don Budge in his Grand Slam year, 1938. In the women's game, Australian women won all but two of the titles, the outsiders being Dorothy Round of Britain (1935) and Dorothy Bundy of America (1938).

One great Australian, with his blend of talent, eccentricity and popularity, embodies the spirit of tennis between the wars: Jack Crawford. He regarded tennis as a gentleman's game wearing long sleeved shirts buttoned at the wrist, played with a flat topped racket (some said to make it easier to sweep the ball up from low positions) and insisted on having a tray with tea, milk and sugar at the umpire's chair. During the customary break after a third set, he disdained the shower and relaxed with a cigarette on court. The crowds loved him.

His tennis was good, too. Although slow and rather lazy about the court Crawford had excellent intuition, and played a placement game from the baseline. He reached five consecutive finals in the Australian championships from 1930, losing one of them, to Fred Perry. During this run he also took the Wimbledon title in 1933 in a classic match against the American cannonball server Ellsworth Vines. He had previously beaten Henri Cochet on the Paris clay, and would have achieved a Grand Slam if Perry had not outlasted him in a five-setter for the US title.

RIGHT: *Fred Perry and Jack Crawford before one of their many gladiatorial contests at Wimbledon.*

ABOVE, FAR RIGHT: *The Worple Road site, which became too small to house the All England Championships as they grew in popularity.*

BELOW: *Tennis had become a major spectator sport by the 1920s, and part of the social 'season' in England.*

Wimbledon Outgrows its Home

Championship tennis returned to Wimbledon in 1919 and public interest in the sport had never been higher. Perhaps fueled by this attention, the game produced some of its great personalities during the interwar years.

It was clear at the first post war tournament that the championships had outgrown their home. Despite improvements made to the Worple Road facilities – including enlarging the stands to hold 3200 people – a move to a more spacious site was required. Everybody – players and spectators – wanted to be at Wimbledon: in 1919 for the first time, ticket applications went into a ballot, and the 128 men's entries exactly met the limit set.

Since the Worple Road site could no longer cope with the championships, a new headquarters in Church Road was commissioned. It was an act of remarkable foresight to opt for such a large site, and one which did much to lay the foundations of the respect which Wimbledon still arouses from players, officials, and crowds alike. The result was the premises that still house the contest every year – although when it was constructed, there was no elegant virginia creeper to disguise the concrete contours of Centre Court; the new All England Lawn Tennis Club was officially opened in 1922 by King George V.

A significant change in the championship format that year abolished the Challenge Round and forced the reigning champions to

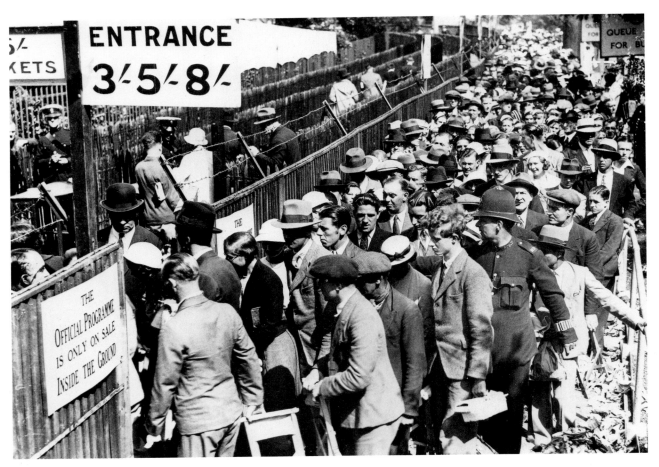

LEFT: *The legendary Wimbledon queue, snapped in 1934. (Some of them may still be there . . .)*

BELOW RIGHT: *London Transport used the popularity of Wimbledon to lure customers on to buses and trains.*

BELOW LEFT: *The Americans and French dominated Wimbledon after the War. Left to right, American Don Budge, Frenchmen Jacques Brugnon, Jean Borotra and Gene Mako, who each won two doubles titles in these pairings.*

battle their way to the final like all the other entrants. Unfortunately, the Cumberland turf (cut near the sea – it still contained some live shrimps) laid for the courts did not stand up well to the demands of tennis, especially as the weather was quite wet, and the muddy tournament took 15 instead of 12 days to complete.

The first match on the new courts featured two British players, Leslie Godfree (who later married Kitty McKane) and Algernon Kingscote. Aware of the historical significance of the occasion, Godfree thumped his first service into the net and started up the court to pick up the ball – the first ball ever hit in competition at the Church Road site. His opponent had similar aspirations, and after a slightly undignified sprint by both players, Godfree had the prize. It was later eaten by moths, who have no sense of history.

The matches played in 1922 included the last appearance by Arthur Gore, who had won the championships three times since he first entered in 1888. Now aged 54, he lost to an Indian living in England, A H Fyzee. Among the newcomers that year were four Frenchmen, Jean Borotra, Jacques Brugnon, Henri Cochet, and

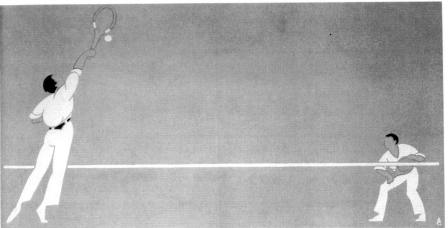

FOR THE WIMBLEDON TOURNAMENT JUNE 25th

NEAREST STATION
SOUTHFIELDS

SPECIAL BUSES TO & FROM
THE STATION AND GROUND

ABOVE: *Jack Crawford walks on court with cannonball server Ellsworth Vines in 1932. Vines went on to win the singles title.*

RIGHT: *Vines' laser-like service created quite a stir, as this contemporary cartoon shows.*

THE UMPIRE BROADCASTS THE POINTS.

VINES V. AOKI
GALVANIZED BY THE FAST PLAY,
THE BALL-BOYS DASH TO THE ICE-BOX
FOR NEW BALLS AND
DRINKS BETWEEN
SETS—

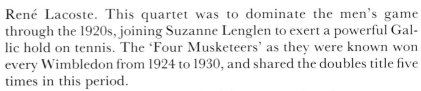

René Lacoste. This quartet was to dominate the men's game through the 1920s, joining Suzanne Lenglen to exert a powerful Gallic hold on tennis. The 'Four Musketeers' as they were known won every Wimbledon from 1924 to 1930, and shared the doubles title five times in this period.

By 1924 a seeding system had been introduced to ensure a balanced draw in which the top players would not meet too early in the competition. In 1925 qualifying contests had to be held for those players who did not earn selection to the 128 permitted entrants in the men's championships. That was the year when all five Wimbledon titles went to France.

1927 was a notable year at Wimbledon, marking the introduction of merit seeding to all events, the first radio broadcasts from the championships, terrible weather which extended the tournament to 14 days, and an amazing semi-finals comeback by Cochet from 2-6, 4-6, 1-5 against the American Bill Tilden. Cochet went on to win the title.

As 1925 had belonged to France, so 1930 – somewhat unexpectedly – belonged to America. At the age of 37 Bill Tilden captured the singles title he first won in 1920, Helen Wills won the women's final, and the only non-American who gained a title was Australian Jack Crawford who partnered Elizabeth Ryan in the mixed doubles.

Two years later, winning the men's singles on his first visit, American Ellsworth Vines earned himself a place in Wimbledon mythology for the service that nobody saw. At championship point against Britain's Bunny Austin, the tall Californian threw the ball up, swung his racket . . . and the next thing anyone knew was the ball thumping into the canvas behind Austin! It was a fitting end to a tournament in which Vines was invincible. He also reached the final in 1933 to face the flamboyant Australian Jack Crawford, who had made a careful study of the American's big serve game. Against all expectations, Crawford proved capable of returning the Vines ser-

ABOVE: *Englishman Bunny Austin, the first man to wear shorts at Wimbledon.*

LEFT: *Dorothy Round, one of the two British singles champions between the wars.*

RIGHT: *German Baron Gottfried von Cramm, who set an unenviable record by losing three consecutive finals.*

ABOVE FAR RIGHT: *Kitty Godfree and Dorothea Lambert Chambers playing doubles at Wimbledon.*

FAR RIGHT: *Champions of two ages – Elizabeth Ryan and Chris Evert, who met at the Wimbledon centenary celebration in 1977.*

vice and, after 100 minutes and 30 games, they stood at two sets all. It was a gladiatorial contest of power against cunning and Crawford eventually won by switching from his baseline game to rush the net, unsettling Vines, who lost his last service game to love. The 4-6, 11-9, 6-2, 2-6, 6-4 final was greeted as a classic, possibly the best-ever match at Wimbledon.

Britain had not had a men's champion since 1909, but in 1934 patriotic fervor was rampant as two Britons – Fred Perry and Dorothy Round – won the singles titles. Fred Perry beat the title-holder Jack Crawford with spectacular, dashing tennis. Crawford was suffering from the mysterious 'Wimbledon throat', a virus that caused 63 withdrawals from the tournament that year. If there was any doubt about Perry's right to the title, it was banished by his two consecutive finals wins over the German Baron Gottfried von Cramm in 1935 and 1936. Perry was the first man to hold the title for three years running since the Challenge Round had been abolished in 1922.

Von Cramm set a more dismal record by being the first man since 1886 to lose three singles finals in a row when he was beaten by the American Don Budge in 1937. Budge won three Wimbledon titles that year, and retained the singles twelve months later without dropping a set. America won all five titles that year, and dominance continued in 1939 when Bobby Riggs snatched the championship at his first attempt.

Women's tennis at Wimbledon matched the men's for excitement and personality clashes, as a succession of very different characters dominated the event. The 1919 tournament saw the dawn of a new era as Suzanne Lenglen made her debut, and won through to the Challenge Round to beat Dorothea Lambert Chambers in one of the most exciting finals ever.

The accomplishments of Lenglen, Alice Marble, Helen Wills, Helen Jacobs and Kitty Godfree are covered in other chapters but one woman earned a place in Wimbledon's hall of fame without ever holding the singles trophy aloft.

Elizabeth Ryan was an American who lived in England, and won 19 doubles titles in 20 years. Six were with Suzanne Lenglen in what was probably the best doubles partnership of all time, and seven

were in the mixed. Ryan weighed 166 pounds, and her chief weapon was an excellent volley behind a chopped forehand approach. If she had not been playing in the company of Lenglen and Wills, she would certainly have added singles honors to her many Wimbledon titles. She took a set off Lenglen in 1924, and must have been particuarly disappointed when the French player won, and then retired sick – not only had she lost in the singles to a player who then defaulted, she had lost her doubles partner too. In 1979, still holder of a record number of Wimbledon titles, she died. The next day Billie Jean King clinched her 20th finals win, and took the record.

1934 was notable for a rare British win in the women's singles, as Dorothy Round defeated Helen Jacobs of America. They were a well-matched pair, and in a tiring match it was all square in the final set when Round, in desperation, abandoned her usual baseline play and, with a series of attacking volleys, won the match. She repeated her victory in 1937, pulling back from a 4-1 deficit in the final set against Poland's Jadwiga Jedrejowska.

A New Face for American Tennis

1920 was an auspicious year for American tennis: it saw the birth of the Wightman Cup, and Bill Tilden won his first singles title, beginning his long domination of tennis both in America and around the globe.

In 1921 work began on new facilities at West Side Tennis Club to create the first permanent tennis stadium in the US, and the men's tournament moved temporarily to Germantown Cricket Club in Philadelphia. Two years later the Forest Hills club unveiled its steel and concrete horseshoe shaped stadium, second only to Wimbledon in size. It had 23 clay and 22 grass courts, and could hold 14,000 people. The first title winner on the court was Helen Wills with the first of seven championship wins, this one over Molla Mallory.

In the same year, the USLTA finally joined the ILTF, which had taken away the political stumbling block by preventing Wimbledon using the title of World Championships for its tournament.

The men's and women's singles tournaments were at last staged at the same venue when the men returned to Forest Hills in 1924, Tilden winning the title before a crowd of 6000. Bill Johnston failed to dethrone him the next year, but the scoreline of 4-6, 11-9, 6-3, 4-6, 6-3 tells its own story of a hard fought, see-sawing match. Tilden's reign over the men's championships ended in 1926 when Henri Cochet beat him in the quarter-finals, and his fellow Musketeers Lacoste and Borotra contested the final, Borotra winning in straight sets.

1929 was a milestone year for the best players of the time, Helen Wills and Bill Tilden. Wills completed a three year run of title wins when she had not dropped a single set in the championships, beating Britain's Phoebe Watson in the final. Tilden notched up his record-equalling seventh title, defeating Francis Hunter. He hated Wills, and was close to her rival Helen Jacobs, so it is unlikely they shared their celebrations. The following year he left the amateur ranks, becoming a pioneer professional. His popularity with the public attracted large crowds, and made the professional circuit more viable for promoters and players alike.

It was drama all the way in 1933. The rival Helens, Wills and Jacobs, met in the final. 3-0 down in the third set, Wills marched off court blaming a back injury and saying she was unable to play. The incident sparked much controversy and fueled the media image of an unsporting duel between the two rivals. In the men's tournament, Australian Jack Crawford seemed poised to complete the first ever Grand Slam (all four major world titles in one year) but was thwarted in a thrilling match by Britain's Fred Perry 6-3, 11-3, 4-6, 6-0, 6-1.

The doubles championships united at the Longwood Cricket Club, Boston, in 1935 where they remained, with the odd exception, until 1967. The same year the USLTA, its coffers bulging from ticket sales and subscriptions, introduced a junior Davis Cup program, for the development of young players, bridging the gap between junior and adult play. It helped produce many future champions, just as the other junior development programs had done since 1917.

FAR LEFT: *Schoolgirl Helen Wills (foreground) on her way to beating Kitty McKane in the new Forest Hills stadium in 1923 . . .*

LEFT: *. . . and in the final, the 17-year-old Californian beat the reigning champion Molla Mallory (right).*

ABOVE: *Bill Tilden in action at Forest Hills in 1925, the year he won his third US title.*

RIGHT: *The baseline strategy of Helen Wills took her to the top of the women's game.*

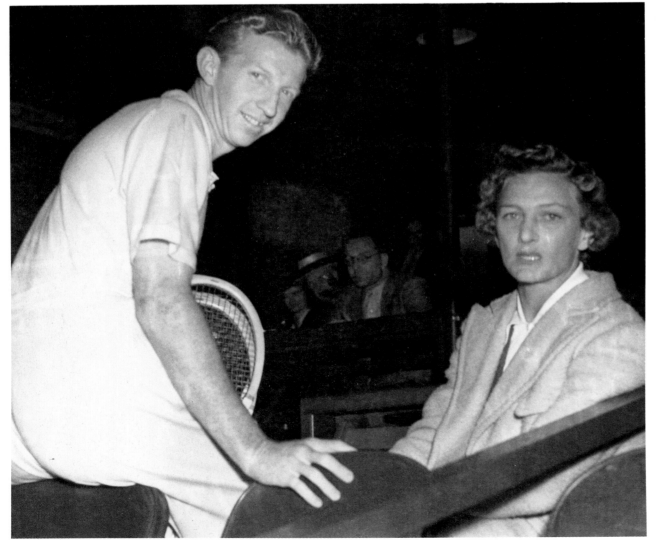

ABOVE LEFT: *Forest Hills, 1933. Jack Crawford (left) walks on court with Fred Perry who beat him, thus preventing Crawford from achieving the first Grand Slam.*

ABOVE: *Don Budge congratulates his doubles partner Gene Mako after their victory on their way to their win in the 1938 US championships.*

LEFT: *Don Budge and Helen Wills Jacobs in 1938.*

ABOVE RIGHT: *Hazel Wightman, who captained the US Olympic team in 1924 and founded the Wightman Cup.*

BELOW RIGHT: *The victorious 1929 American Wightman Cup team.*

Alice Marble was leading women's tennis at this time, and an American had always made it to the singles finals, but in 1937 US championship spectators were shocked to find a Pole and a Chilean meet for the title. South American Anita Lizana beat Jadwiga Jedrzejowska in straight sets, and to the crowd's astonishment, both players then hugged and kissed on court.

Marble grabbed the title back in a 22 minute final next year, but 1938 is best remembered for Don Budge's historic first Grand Slam, clinched by defeating Gene Mako 6-3, 6-8, 6-2, 6-1. Budge promptly turned professional, part of a procession of major title holders who broke with the shamateurism of top tennis in the 1930s and tried to make a more honest living.

Wartime traveling restrictions forced the five major championships into one venue, Forest Hills, from 1942 to 1946. The USLTA had previously kept the doubles and singles contests separate to spread tennis interest as wide as possible.

The Wightman Cup was donated to the USLTA in 1920 by Hazel Wightman (neé Hotchkiss), an accomplished tennis player, and was intended as the trophy for an annual Women's Lawn Tennis Team Championship between Great Britain and the United States – a sort of women's small-scale Davis Cup. The format, then as now, was five singles and two doubles matches, the venue alternating every year. The trophy is an elaborately decorated silver vase, 24in (61cm) high. It was first contested in 1923 at the new Forest Hills stadium, and the strong American team of Hazel Wightman, Molla Mallory, Helen Wills, and Eleanor Goss trounced the British (Kitty McKane, Mrs A E Beamish, Mrs R C Clayton, and Mrs B C Covell) by winning all seven matches. Although honors were even up to 1930, America has continued to hold a powerful grip on the trophy ever since, but even if some of the matches were one sided, they proved popular with the public – nearly 3000 spectators watched the first contest, and until recent years, it continued to attract a sizeable audience. Today the contest has become an irrelevance to international tennis, and has been consistently downgraded. Even teams of American juniors are able to comfortably defeat the best Britain can offer, and such dominance breeds boredom on court and in the stands.

The Davis Cup goes International

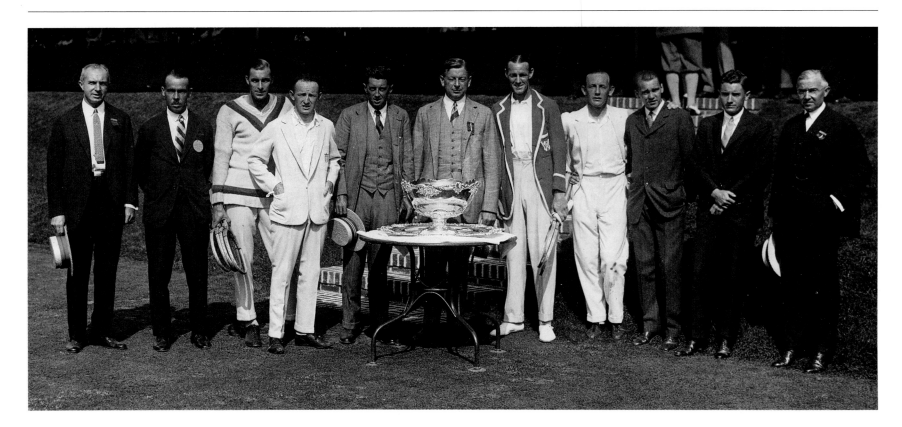

After the First World War America declined to challenge Australia for the Davis Cup as the USA had suffered fewer losses than other countries; nevertheless the competition continued.

By 1921 the original trophy had run out of room for names of new winners, and Dwight Davis donated a solid silver tray – good enough for another 15 years, after which Davis came up with a circular base for both tray and bowl. In the interwar years, the Davis Cup contributed to the 'Golden Age' of tennis by creating a stream of exciting matches played to full houses by major stars (some of whom however were to opt for professionalism – which meant leaving the Davis Cup).

The number of entrants each year rose steadily, leading in 1923 to the division of the challengers into European and American zones, with an inter-zone final deciding who should challenge the Davis Cup holder. Countries could select which zone to contest, and the majority, including the South Americans, opted for Europe partly because the USA was so strong and partly because the Davis Cup ties coincided with Wimbledon.

Countries such as India and Japan began to mount serious challenges in their zones, which was evidence both of the growing popularity of tennis around the world, and of the attraction of the Davis Cup as a national prize. However, the holding nation retained a tremendous advantage in being able to watch challengers as they fought through for the right to the final tie, and in selecting the surface on which the matches would be played.

1920 saw the beginning of six years' dominance of the Davis Cup by America, led by the remarkable Bill Tilden. Japan won through to meet America in the 1921 final, and Zenzo Shimizu, a crafty, unorthodox player with a superb lob, came close to defeating Bill Tilden who was ill and had a foot injury. Tilden had won only one of the three sets played when the players took their then customary break. While Shimizu waited for the re-start, Tilden collapsed fully dressed in the shower. But the refreshing water and lancing the boil on his foot revitalized him. Back on court, the Japanese man suffered from cramp, probably because he had not showered or massaged his legs, and an exhausted Tilden won the day, contributing to America's retention of the cup.

The French built up a formidable team during the mid-1920s and in 1927 captured the Davis Cup, keeping it by beating the Americans

five times and the British once in the challenge rounds for the next six years. A crucial match in that first win over America was Lacoste vs Tilden. Tilden had already played a doubles game and been involved in bickering in the American camp. The Frenchman, 11 years younger, exhausted his opponent by playing a wide variety of angles and paces in his shots, moving him around the court. Tilden commented that Lacoste was so accurate and consistent that he felt he had been playing a machine.

Tilden's battles with Lacoste, Cochet and Borotra, especially in the Davis Cup, fascinated tennis crowds over these years, and there was great consternation in France in 1928 when Tilden was banned from the visiting American team because of alleged professionalism.

Controversy returned in 1932 when the USA was fancied to regain the Davis Cup and much depended on the fourth match in the tie, between Borotra and the Texan Wilmer Allison. The Americans were never happy on the slow, dampened, French clay courts, and indeed the court did not much suit the net rusher Borotra either. Borotra had saved two match points, and changed his shoes twice, when on the third match point, he delighted the French crowd by sitting on a ballboy's back and sucking an orange while two more ballboys changed his shoes yet again. Riled by what they considered to be gamesmanship, the America team could hardly believe what happened as Borotra faced a fourth match point. After netting his first service, Borotra's second serve looked well out. Allison slashed the ball away as he began to celebrate victory – but heard no call from the line judge. Despite the booing of French fans, who saw the injustice, the officials did not relent. Allison won only one more point and the deciding set was lost 5-7. The episode resulted in a tightening up of rules of surface preparation, the number of people allowed on court, and the temperature the balls were kept at.

In the end it was the British who wrested the cup from French hands, due in part to the skills of Fred Perry. They kept the trophy for four years – a repeat of the feat by the Doherty brothers earlier in the century.

1937 saw America defeat Germany in the inter-zone final for the right to challenge a British team depleted by the loss of Perry to the professional game; much of the credit for their win goes to the immortal Don Budge. Australia challenged unsuccessfully the following year, but won the cup in 1939, partly thanks to American Bobby

Riggs pulling a stomach muscle at match point down against the elder, very experienced and talented Adrian Quist.

Dwight Davis was unable to attend the draw that year – he was busy gathering up his family in Europe and ensuring they got home before the inevitable war. Nazism cast a shadow over tennis as it did over everything else in the 1930s. Jews were forbidden to play in the German teams, and the international tennis community rarely complained. An exception to this was a letter to *The Times* in 1933, from Fred Perry and Bunny Austin: 'We have always valued our participation in international sport because we believed it to be a great opportunity for the promotion of better international understanding and because it was a human activity that contained no distinction of race, class or creed.'

FAR LEFT: *The successful Americans with the Australian Davis Cup team of 1923.*

ABOVE: *Evidence of growing internationalism came when Japan entered the Davis Cup in 1929. John Hennessey is beating Japan's Tanio Abe . . .*

LEFT: *. . . and Yoshira Ohta and John Van Ryan met in the same rubber.*

RIGHT: *Germany's Von Cramm (who once received an encouraging call from the Führer before a match) smashes a lob during the tie with America in 1937.*

The Showman

He died alone at the age of 60, his bags packed for a Cleveland tournament, a legend with few friends. The Bill Tilden story is tinged with sadness, for Tilden was a lonely figure throughout his life. No one then or since has come close to understanding the complex nature of one of the greatest players and tacticians in the history of tennis.

Born into a rich Philadelphia family in 1893, Bill Tilden had an unhappy childhood, and in tennis terms was a late developer, serving a long apprenticeship playing mixed doubles (his partners included Molla Mallory and Mary K Browne). He did not win his first major title until he was 27, when he beat Australian Gerald Patterson in the Wimbledon challenge final, and became the first American to win Wimbledon. He did not lose another match of significance for six years, saving a match point to retain his Wimbledon title the next year, and sweeping the US singles championship from 1920 to 1925.

Tilden had a very fast serve – once clocked at more than 150mph, about the same speed as Becker's today – and ran the game from the baseline, shunting his opponent around the court, and occasionally venturing to the net to display his volleying skills. He perfected just about every stroke in the book, giving him an unheard of variety of shots. He wrote articles and books theorizing about the chess-like strategy of tennis, and was a perfectionist about his game. He remodeled his backhand after a loss to Bill Johnston (dubbed 'Little Bill') in 1919, and had to modify his grip in 1922 after losing the tip of a finger when he ran into some wire netting.

Tilden came to Forest Hills in 1920 as Wimbledon champion to face his more popular rival Bill Johnston. About 10,000 people packed into the wooden stands at the club to watch the final. At two sets all, a military plane taking aerial photographs plunged to the ground, missing the court by 100 yards. Both occupants died, but the players agreed to continue the match to help avert panic in the crowd. Tilden won, as he did each time the same pair met in five subsequent finals.

But whoever big Bill Tilden played, the match was never one sided. He loved to please the crowd, allowing his opponent a head start before suddenly raising his game for a spectacular recovery. Tilden had a particularly icy glare for linesmen who displeased him, and reveled in the sense of drama he created. He would sometimes serve out the match by starting the game with five balls in his hand, and wallop four cannonball aces before disdainfully tossing away the surplus ball. He was also a scrupulous sportsman, deliberately netting balls if he felt his opponent had been wronged by a line decision, and applauding good shots with a cry of 'peach!' The crowds adored him, and 'Big Bill' relished the attention.

Tilden was the master of tennis in every tournament he chose to enter until 1926, when a knee injury cost him a victory. He beat his early rival Bill Johnston for all but one of his US titles, and teamed up with him to win the Davis Cup from Australia in 1920, helping to keep it in America with a run of 13 successive wins in the challenge round from 1920 to 1926. In his ten year Davis Cup career, he won 34 rubbers out of 41. With his excellent doubles and mixed play, he

BELOW LEFT: *Bill Tilden cut an elegant figure on court and off.*

ABOVE LEFT: *Tilden with his last US singles cup in 1929.*

ABOVE: *The two Bills, Johnston and Tilden. They fought seven consecutive US finals, Johnston only* *winning the first in 1919. Little Bill was more popular with the crowds than his tall, patrician rival.*

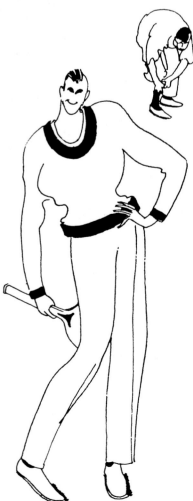

amassed 16 US titles, and won the Wimbledon doubles too, with Frank Hunter in 1927, when they saved a match point in the final. He always struggled in the French championships, where he lost a number of key matches to Lacoste and Cochet. In 1929, aged 36 Tilden took his seventh US title, going on to win easily at Wimbledon the following year after an amazing five set semi-final against Jean Borotra. The next year he turned professional and dominated that arena too, playing exhibition matches in Madison Square Garden, and winning the US Pro title in 1931 and 1935.

Bill Tilden was eccentric, shy, and isolated in a society which did not tolerate his sexuality and in the early years of his career rooted for the small, gutsy Bill Johnston against the tall, patrician Tilden. His homosexuality led to two jail terms for indecency offences in later years, and he lost many of his friends as a result. No one represented the tennis authorities at his funeral service. He was a mentor of Molla Mallory and Helen Jacobs, but had few close friends. One of the ironies of his life was that he yearned for recognition less on the tennis court than on the stage. He backed numerous shows, and was disappointed at the lack of acclaim his (apparently very amateurish) acting attracted. However, he is remembered as one the best players of and thinkers about the game, being ranked top in many surveys of the best players in the history of tennis.

LEFT: *Occasionally posturing and with a love of drama, Tilden's elegant manner aroused the interest of the sketch artist from the* Illustrated London News *in 1921.*

RIGHT: *Tilden mastered every stroke and was a keen student of tennis strategy. Note the spare ball in his hand. Sometimes he took five, served four aces, and ostentatiously threw the superfluous ball to the sideline.*

The Queen of Tennis

Suzanne Lenglen became celebrated for her formidable play and temperament, and she opened up a new era in the game with her highly charged, brilliant tennis. She also earned a reputation as a temperamental prima donna – and the crowds loved her for it.

Born in May 1899 into a poor family, Lenglen used to practise her tennis constantly in an age where such dedication was not really expected. She was helped by the Wimbledon champion Dorothea Lambert Chambers and developed a strong baseline style that depended on the accuracy of her groundstrokes. She was also very quick on her dainty feet, dancing round the court showing excellent anticipation. If pressed she also played well at the net.

The Frenchwoman was always very close to her father Charles, who acted as a Svengali-like figure until he died in 1928. In the early days he used to place handkerchiefs on the court for her to hit to test out the accuracy of her shots.

Lenglen made her Wimbledon debut at the age of 20, and fought through to the final to meet her childhood coach, Mrs Lambert Chambers. Lenglen saved two set points in the first set before winning it 10-8. She lost the second, and faced two match points in the final set. A lucky shot off the frame, followed by a perfect backhand, saved the points, and she dramatically won 9-7. She never faced a match point again in her entire playing career. Lenglen defeated Lambert Chambers much more convincingly in 1920, and won the women's and mixed doubles too – the first ever triple crown at Wimbledon, and a feat she repeated in 1922 and 1925. She went on to win all three events in the French national championships from 1919 to 1923, recovering from illness to regain the triple crown in 1925 and 1926.

When Lenglen was on court, drama was never far away. Playing the American champion Molla Mallory in the 1921 World Hard Court final in Paris, she faced an important break point in the second set. Suddenly she stopped, claiming she had a pain in her feet and that she must retire. She was persuaded to continue and won the

RIGHT: *Helen Wills (right), beautiful but prim – a complete contrast to the vivacious fur-coated pose of Suzanne Lenglen.*

LEFT: *Suzanne Lenglen insisted on wearing calf-length cotton for easy movement, attire that was considered risqué in 1919.*

ABOVE: *Lenglen's dynamic play always amazed the crowds, particularly at a time when women players were expected to play with more decorum than energy.*

ABOVE: *Lenglen swoops across the court to return another unlikely shot.*

ABOVE RIGHT: *Her wardrobe always attracted interest, especially this one-piece culotte suit with detachable shirt.*

match, but this was not the last occasion when Suzanne Lenglen claimed illness at times of pressure. In the American championships of 1921 Lenglen again faced Molla Mallory. The Frenchwoman suffered from asthma and the sea voyage to the U S had not been easy. A set and 2-0 down, she retired and left the court in tears, much to the anger of the crowd. Her American tour was canceled and she never returned. However, she subsequently beat Molla Mallory several times, once in the final at Wimbledon.

Although not a beauty, Suzanne Lenglen had a marvelous figure and was a stylish dresser, sporting a colored bandeau which added to her aura of glamour and was quickly copied by other women. She would often arrive on court dressed in a fur coat, removing it to reveal a one-piece, calf-length cotton dress that was considered very revealing at the time. She resented other players getting public attention, and guarded her status at Wimbledon ruthlessly. Once she found someone else's clothes in her room and threw them out of a window . . . before she discovered that they belonged to Elizabeth Ryan, her best friend!

Lenglen reigned supreme at Wimbledon, winning five consecutive singles championships from 1919. Everyone wanted to beat her, but only one player seemed equipped to do it: Helen Wills, the steady, hard hitting American. They finally met in Cannes in February, 1926. The Frenchwoman won the first set 6-3, but was sipping medicinal brandy between games of the second set, and the American kept coming back at her. Lenglen called on her volley to see her through and eventually emerged the winner at 8-6. She immediately burst into tears. The pair never played again.

The same year saw an undignified exit from Wimbledon. Due to play in the singles and then the doubles in front of Queen Mary, Lenglen arrived late, and was rebuked by the referee. Amid great histrionics, she refused to play. In the mixed doubles three days later, the crowd showed her the disapproval they felt for their former darling, and she retired from the championships.

Lenglen spent two unhappy years as a professional playing exhibition matches and retained her unbeaten record – since 1914 she had not lost a singles match. She became a successful coach until her death from leukemia in July 1938. She had occupied a uniquely theatrical place in tennis history, was adored by the French crowds, and was posthumously awarded the Cross of the Legion of Honour.

BELOW: *Leaps like this were a Lenglen trademark.*

BELOW RIGHT: *Curtseying to Queen Mary in 1926, the year of Lenglen's dramatic exit from Wimbledon.*

A Plucky Champion

Kitty Godfree was one of only two British women to win Wimbledon between the wars. A fine all round sportswoman, she also played hockey and badminton, but was unfortunate in that her prowess at tennis coincided with a period of early excellence in the women's game – her chief rivals were Suzanne Lenglen and Helen Wills.

Born Kathleen McKane in May 1896, she was a fit child, for by the age of ten she had cycled with her family the 600 miles from Kensington to Berlin – the McKane family took their sport seriously! By 1920 the talented youngster had forced her way into the British tennis team for the Olympic Games in Antwerp, winning a gold medal in the doubles, a silver in the mixed and a bronze in the singles.

The same year she began a run of successive All England badminton titles, showing her aptitude for the sport during her winter breaks from tennis.

In 1924 Godfree met 18-year-old Helen Wills in the Wimbledon final, and soon faced a deficit of 6-4, 4-1 and 40-15. But she made one of the remarkable recoveries which were her trademark, and began rushing the net to counteract her powerful opponent's groundstrokes. When she finally clinched victory the crowd went mad celebrating the first British win for ten years. It was the last time any player beat Helen Wills in the Wimbledon singles. She was trounced by Lenglen in the French Open finals and the semi-finals at Wimbledon the next year, but the French tennis queen withdrew in 1926, and the Briton beat Senorita Lili de Alvarez, the Spanish champion, to regain her title. She also won the mixed doubles championship, partnered by the man she had just married, Leslie Godfree. They are

ABOVE: *Kitty Godfree (left) sporting a similar bandeau to that popularized by Suzanne Lenglen (right).*

BELOW: *Godfree meets George V at the 1927 Wimbledon Jubilee celebrations.*

RIGHT: *A determined Godfree during her 1926 Wimbledon finals win over Lili de Alvarez, this time favoring the style of visor worn by Helen Wills.*

ABOVE: *Kitty Godfree partnered by her husband Leslie; they won the Wimbledon mixed title in 1926.*

RIGHT: *Godfree meets the Duchess of Kent in 1986.*

FAR RIGHT: *Godfree the battler prepares a forehand smash. How much stronger would it have been if she had been allowed to play left-handed?*

the only married couple to have won the mixed doubles at Wimbledon.

Kitty Godfree captured one major title away from England: the doubles in the US National Championships in 1923. She was, however, in the winning British Wightman cup teams of 1924, 1925 and 1930. In those first two years she defeated Helen Wills four times in singles and doubles, but she lost to the great American in the US National Championships final in 1925.

Wimbledon prizes were £5 vouchers for the jewelers Mappin & Webb in those days, arriving in the post after the tournament. Kitty saved £80-worth and bought a diamond ring, which she then sold to purchase a green two seater open car. She was concerned this would affect her amateur status and kept this secret from the family for 60

years. Kitty stayed true to the amateur spirit of the game, saying the only coaching she ever had was from uncles and cousins when she first started playing tennis at the age of ten. They forced her to play right-handed, despite her natural left-handedness. If they had not been so strict, perhaps she would have been an even better player.

Her style was quick and aggressive, and she had the athleticism and match play instincts to pull herself back from the brink of defeat many times. The last tournament Kitty Godfree played in was the 1935 covered court championship at the Queens Club, London, at the age of 39. She continued playing for fun on the courts of Wimbledon until she was 89. In 1986 she presented the winners' singles trophies at the Paris and Wimbledon tournaments.

The Two Helens

One of the most famous incidents at Forest Hills occured in 1935, when the two Helens, Wills and Jacobs, faced each other for the championship. Wills, down 0-3 in the final set, was in obvious pain from a back injury. She approached the umpire and told him she would have to default the match. Her opponent put a hand on her shoulder and said 'Won't you rest a while, Helen?' The gesture was rejected coldly: 'Take you hand off my shoulder,' and Helen Wills stalked off the court. Five years later, as Helen Wills achieved a record eighth win in the Wimbledon singles, the crowd was strangely indifferent to the achievement. Her opponent, Helen Jacobs, was in much pain from a foot injury, and asked if she could interrupt play to remove her bandage. Receiving no reply from the other side of the net, she did take it off, ignoring her opponent's stony silence. As Jacobs limped uncomfortably through the second set, winning not one game, the crowd turned as cool towards Wills as she was to her rival.

The incidents highlighted the rivalry of the two Helens, who were the top American women players of the 1930s. Both from Berkeley, California, and both classically beautiful, they dogged each other for years in a long-standing feud that made for some dramatic tennis.

Helen Wills was the better player overall. If Suzanne Lenglen added a new elegant dimension to tennis, Helen Wills took it a step further with her cool, determined play that marked her out as a win-

LEFT: *Helen Jacobs (left) and Helen Wills disliked each other and conducted an infamous rivalry.*

ABOVE RIGHT: *Still nursing her injured ankle, Jacobs congratulates Wills after their 1938 final. Wills remains indifferent.*

BELOW: *Single-minded determination and an excellent array of shots helped Wills take on Lenglen's mantle as the top woman player.*

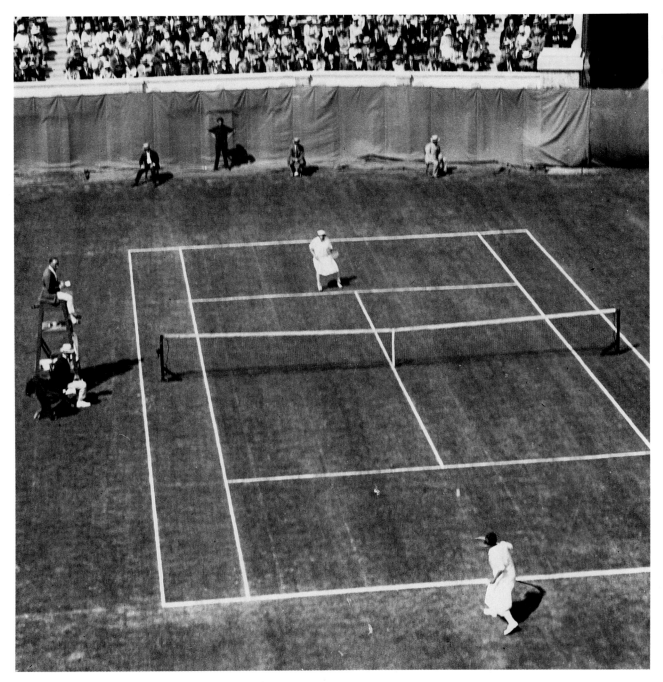

LEFT: *Wills (at net) takes revenge for the 1922 US finals defeat by Molla Mallory, by beating her the following year.*

BELOW LEFT: *Wills at her peak in 1929, walks on court where she trounced Mallory without losing a game.*

ner from the start. Born in 1905, she was a lively child who developed a deep love of the game. In her teens she copied Bill Johnston's heavy forehand drive to create a stroke that was to crush the spirit of many an opponent. By the age of 16 she was in the final of the National Singles Championship, losing to Molla Mallory, who defeated her four times that year (1922). In 1923 she won the title, but did not travel to Europe to meet the famous Suzanne Lenglen as she wanted to complete her studies at the University of California.

Wills had massive self-confidence, but was also a perfectionist and was highly critical of her own play. On court, she showed little emotion, (unlike Suzanne Lenglen) earning the nickname 'Little Miss Poker Face', and therefore did not endear herself to the crowd.

When Lenglen departed from the amateur tennis scene, Wills took over the top spot, winning eight Wimbledon singles titles, seven more in America (dropping only one set in all seven finals) and four in France. From 1927 to 1932 she won every major singles championship, except Australia, never losing a set in singles play. She also won doubles titles at least once in each of these countries. She was triple champion in the US championships twice, in 1924 and 1928, teamed with Hazel Wightman in the ladies doubles and Vivian Richards and John Hawkes in the mixed, but was not able to repeat the feat at Wimbledon. Wills was also successful in the Wightman Cup, playing in the contest nine times and losing only twice in the singles. Her eight wins in the Wimbledon singles were equalled by Martina Navratilova in 1987.

Perhaps her ruthless, power-driving play, combined with a cool, detached manner, accounts for her lack of popularity with tennis crowds of the time. Wills did not mix much with her tennis-playing colleagues, but developed many interests outside tennis, and pur-

sued a career as a painter and writer. Among her friends were the British politician Stanley Baldwin, the painter Augustus John, and the author George Bernard Shaw. Helen Wills married to become Helen Moody, and from 1938, Mrs Helen Roark.

Helen Jacobs was nearly three years younger than her rival. They lived a few blocks apart in Berkeley, and William Fuller of the local Berkeley Lawn Tennis Club introduced them and suggested they play a practice set. Wills clobbered her opponent 6-0 in seven minutes, in the first of many clashes.

Jacobs divided her time between her studies and tennis, and in 1924 clinched the National Junior Championship, impressing Bill Tilden with her ability to play well under stress. In fact she had worked hard to control her turbulent temperament and taught herself a self-discipline that came more naturally to Helen Wills.

In 1928 the two Helens met in the American championship final, and the younger player's weak forehand was exposed by her skilful opponent. Jacobs later won the tournament four times in succession from 1932, losing to Alice Marble in the finals for the following two years. In 1934 she won the triple crown of singles, doubles and mixed at Forest Hills.

She only won Wimbledon once in five finals, her victory in 1936 followed great disappointment the year before, when she missed an easy volley at championship point and went on to lose the next five games and the match to . . . Helen Wills. Jacobs was always in the shadow of her fellow American, and was runner-up to her in many tournaments. A modest, intelligent woman who earned great popularity from the crowds, she wrote various books about tennis, and is remembered for her tenacity, her sportsmanship, and her rivalry around the globe with the woman who haunted her tennis life.

Jacobs was more workmanlike than her rival, and showed greater tenacity. TOP: *stooping for a low volley.* ABOVE: *stretching for a high return.*

The Four Musketeers

The 'Four Musketeers', Jean Borotra, Jacques Brugnon, Henri Cochet, and René Lacoste, came from nowhere to add to the efforts of Suzanne Lenglen in making France the dominant tennis nation of the 1920s. Between them they kept the French singles title from 1924 to 1932, the Wimbledon singles from 1924 to 1929, as well as three US singles titles. They won 120 of their 164 Davis Cup rubbers, winning the Cup for France from 1927 to 1932. Although they were very different characters, they were friends as well as rivals, and together provide one of the most extraordinary passages in tennis history.

The eldest, born in 1895, was Jacques 'Toto' Brugnon. Never as strong in singles play as the others, he was a superlative doubles player, being a great positioner of the ball and the best exponent of the attacking lob the game has seen. Usually paired with Cochet, he won 11 doubles and five mixed titles in his career.

Younger by three years was Jean Borotra, who first picked up a tennis racket when he was 13 on holiday in England. He became an unorthodox player, no stylist, but highly athletic, very determined, and an early master of the serve-volley game. Extrovert and mischevious, he was known as the 'Bounding Basque', because of his energy and his birthplace on the Basque coast. His trademark was a succession of berets lined up neatly by the umpire's chair. Crowds cheered as he donned the first, then regularly swapped it for the next

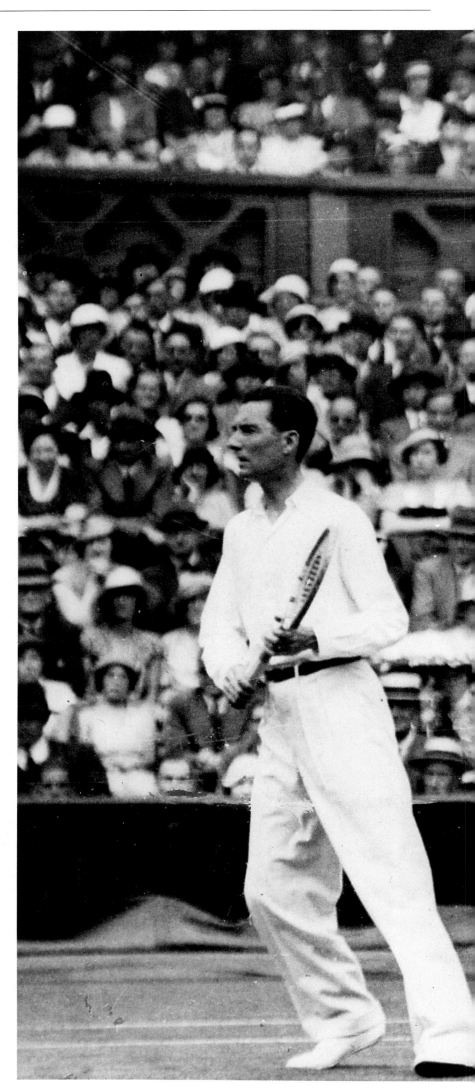

LEFT: *René Lacoste (left) and Jean Borotra, Wimbledon 1924.*

BELOW: *Jacques Brugnon stays serene as Borotra leaps for a smash. The Four Musketeers frequently partnered each other in doubles play.*

ABOVE: *Typical Borotra antics: a showy fall (top left) and collapsing on to a linesman – no doubt the intended target.*

LEFT: *Henri Cochet, a stylish and imaginative player, but prone to horrible errors.*

BELOW RIGHT: *Borotra and Lacoste (background) challenge Williams and Washburn of the US in 1924.*

in line as the match progressed. If one of his famous lobs set up a smash for his opponent, he would sprint in the wrong direction and leap into the crowd as if to escape the cannonball, making sure he landed in a pretty girl's lap. Borotra won the French and Wimbledon singles twice, and the Australian singles once, also acquiring nine doubles and five mixed titles.

Henri Cochet was born in 1901, son of the secretary of the Lyons tennis club, where he was a ballboy in his youth. A small man, he was not a powerful player, but had marvelous anticipation and perfected the art of striking the ball early, on the rise. It was a technique copied by Fred Perry, and more recently used by Jimmy Connors, for its capacity to hurry and ruffle an opponent. The most gifted of the Four Musketeers, master of the volley and half volley, Cochet was an enigmatic character prone to sudden losses of form. He won five French, two Wimbledon and one US singles title, plus a number of doubles championships.

The youngest musketeer, René Lacoste, was born in 1904 and would probably have become one of the greatest names ever in tennis if he had not been dogged by ill health and forced into retirement before he was 25. A fanatical note taker, he studied his contemporaries carefully, which helped him become a shrewd tactician. He wore down his opponents with astute ground strokes, his persistence earning him the nickname 'the crocodile'. (He later used a crocodile symbol on his famous clothing range.) Lacoste was three times singles champion in France, and won two Wimbledon and US titles. A measure of his tactical shrewdness is that he beat another deep thinker on tennis, Bill Tilden, several times, including victories in 1927 for the Wimbledon and US championships.

The Davis Cup was considered the most important tennis event during this period, and from 1923 the 'Four Musketeers' were united in the French team. They lost two Challenge Rounds before defeating America in 1927, when Lacoste beat the two Bills, Johnston and Tilden in vital rubbers. France held the Cup for six years. A venue at which to defend it was required, and thus the Stade Roland Garros was completed in 1928, where the USA and Britain (once) fell victim to the stylish French team.

The 'Four Musketeers' became tennis legends. A few incidents illustrate their charm. In 1924 Borotra met Lacoste in a Wimbledon final played at a furious pace, each of the five sets taking only about 15 minutes. After Borotra's 6-1, 3-6, 6-1, 3-6, 6-4 victory the French pair left the court arm in arm, to the delight of the crowd.

Three years later, Borotra lost to Cochet in the Wimbledon final

4-6, 4-6, 6-3, 6-4, 7-5. Amazingly, Cochet had recovered from two sets down in the quarter and semi-finals too, the latter match against Bill Tilden. He is the only player to have won Wimbledon after such a deficit in the three final rounds. Even in 1939, Brugnon and Borotra were a formidable doubles pair, losing the French final 10-8 in the fifth set.

The 'Four Musketeers' took French and world tennis by storm, and their fraternity and sense of humor contributed to their tremendous popularity with tennis fans of the 1920s.

The Great Competitor

LEFT: *Alice Marble (left) with Caroline Babcock in 1936, the year Marble won her first US singles title.*

Alice Marble was a formidable tennis player, in her time probably the best there had ever been, who based her game on aggression and the will to win. Her career was interrupted first by illness, and then by the Second World War, just when she was at the height of her powers.

Born into a large, fairly poor San Francisco family in 1913, Alice Marble first picked up a tennis racket at the age of 15. It was supplied by her brother Dan who felt she was too much of a tomboy and ought to take up a ladylike game. Marble thrived on practice on the Californian cement courts, developing an all-round game in which serving and volleying played a more important part than was common at that time. But she had much to learn about the grass court game still favored on the East Coast, and took on Eleanor 'Teach' Tennant as her coach. By 1932 she was among the top ten players in America, and in the next year represented the USA in the Wightman Cup. But with a promising tennis career ahead of her, she faced a new battle with terrible illness. Following a dramatic on-court collapse in Paris, tuberculosis was diagnosed, and she was told she would never play tennis again.

Resting in a California sanatorium, Marble was greatly encouraged by a supportive letter from the film star Carole Lombard, and forced herself into a recovery, despite the fact that for five months she was not even allowed to walk. In 1936, in spite of official doubts about her fitness, Alice Marble competed in and won the US singles

championships at Forest Hills. In the final she met Helen Jacobs. After losing the first set, she began to play more aggressively, attacking her opponent's forehand from the net, and rushing in behind her service. The tactic paid off, and she clinched the match with a powerful smash.

Marble built up an impressive tally of titles over the next few years. She won the US singles championship again in 1938, 1939 and 1940, and she and partner Sarah Palfrey Fabyan pulled off the doubles four times in a row from 1937 to 1940. In the mixed doubles, she won with Gene Mako (1936), Don Budge (1938), Harry Hopman (1939), and Bobby Riggs (1940). She thus achieved the triple crown in the US championships for three successive years. Marble also won three titles at Wimbledon in 1939, a feat which only Lenglen had achieved before. She had won the mixed doubles twice in the preceding years, partnered with Don Budge, and in 1938 had won the ladies doubles with Fabyan.

She finally got the singles title after two years of losing in the semifinal. This time she ruthlessly defeated the British player Kay Stammers (who had previously taught her how to apply make-up to appear less pale after her terrible illness). Alice Marble set a new standard in women's tennis which many contemporaries tried to emulate. In 1941 she turned professional; she was later to help instil in Billie Jean King that desire to win which had marked her out during so much of her own career.

ABOVE: *Marble was a brilliant serve-volleyer, whose career was interrupted by illness.*

RIGHT: *Helen Jacobs (left) and Alice Marble met in the 1936 US final. Marble won 4-6, 6-3, 6-2.*

RIGHT: *A picture of concentration, Alice Marble in action at Wimbledon in 1937, when she won the mixed title with Don Budge.*

The People's Champion

LEFT: *In 1933 Fred Perry of Britain met Australia's Jack Crawford in the US final, only the second time two foreign players had met at this stage.*

RIGHT: *Perry executes a crisp forehand. Competitive and resourceful, Perry studied his fellow players and exploited their weaknesses.*

BELOW: *Perry and Crawford chat before a match.*

In 1934, when Fred Perry had just become the first Englishman to win the Wimbledon men's singles for 25 years, he lay relaxing in the dressing room bath, and heard a Club Committee man consoling his defeated opponent Jack Crawford: 'This was one day when the best man didn't win'. The official gave Crawford a bottle of champagne, and left the room without speaking to the new champion, silently dropping his newly earned club tie on to a chair. The snub typifies Perry's career: viewed from the Wimbledon towers as an upstart with the wrong background, he was often out of step with authority, but still a winner through and through.

Born in Stockport, Cheshire in 1909 and educated in west London, Perry was the son of a Labour MP. This was not the background of the typical British tennis player of the time. A good all-round athlete, he was a world table tennis champion before taking up tennis seriously.

Perry moved about the court fast on his long legs and hit the ball unusually early, modeling his game on Henri Cochet. He had a whiplash forehand drive, and loved to get to the net behind this stroke or his big service. A determined, resourceful player, Perry used to research the strengths and weaknesses of his opponents carefully in advance, and refused to shake hands with anyone before a match, for fear of injuring his right hand.

He made winning the first set a top priority in any match, reasoning that it provided an excellent head start, and forced good opponents into longer, more tiring, matches. Perry was very fit and prided himself on not losing five-set matches. Always keen to gain an advantage, he used the ten minute break which always followed the first three sets to change from his deliberately off-white tennis clothes into a brilliantly white set, carefully parted his hair, and reappeared before his opponent a vision of composure.

LEFT: *Perry in 1934, when he clinched his first Wimbledon title.*

RIGHT: *Perry commiserates with von Cramm after winning the 1935 final; he repeated the result the following year.*

Perry made his first impact by helping Britain defeat France to win the Davis Cup in 1933, beating his hero Henri Cochet in a grueling five setter 8-10, 6-4, 8-6, 3-6, 6-1. In the deciding rubber he defied the French crowd by beating André Merlin, and led Britain to win the Davis Cup for the first time since 1912. Thousands greeted the team on its arrival back in London, hoisting Perry and his teammates on to their shoulders and carrying them out of the station in triumph.

Later that year Perry reached the US national finals and faced Jack Crawford, who was out to complete the first ever Grand Slam. Crawford played from the baseline, and Perry's tactics against such opponents were to play a waiting game, allowing the other player to make the first mistake. Crawford had been kept late the previous evening winning his semi-final, and Perry exploited his fatigue to take the match 6-3, 11-13, 4-6, 6-0, 6-1. The victory began a period of three years in which Perry won 13 Grand Slam titles, in an era when the standard of tennis was high and rising all the time.

The pair met again in the Wimbledon final the next year, Perry winning on a Crawford double fault after 70 minutes. He performed a delighted cartwheel before his customary victory vault of the net, but the anticlimactic service fault end to the match was curiously symbolic of his lack of popularity with the Wimbledon authorities.

Perry went on to retain his US title, beating Wilmer Allison 8-6 in the final set. Everywhere he went, he was asked if he was following the now customary route of major title holders and turning professional. The pressure got heavier the next year as he won the French title (for the first time) and Wimbledon, on both occasions beating Baron von Cramm in the finals. Since he had won the Australian Open in 1934, Perry now became the first player to have picked up every grand slam trophy. He set his targets on a third successive Wimbledon title, and in the end won with ease over an injured von Cramm. Typically, Perry knew from a masseur's tip-off of the German's injury, and ruthlessly played to his weakness, ending the match in 40 minutes.

Almost immediately, Perry led Britain to its fourth Davis Cup win in succession, this time over Australia. It was the last time he played in Britain's Davis Cup team: soon he joined the ranks of ex-All England Club members by turning pro. Teamed up with players such as Ellsworth Vines and Bill Tilden, he joined the whirlwind of exhibition matches around the world, and won the US Pro title in 1938 and 1941.

In 1984 the All England Club commemorated the 50th anniversary of his first title by putting up a statue of him and renaming the south eastern gate the Fred Perry Gate. It represented recognition of a player who the public loved but whose face did not fit with the tennis establishment.

The First Grand Slam

Don Budge was the first player to win all the Grand Slam singles titles (Australian, French, Wimbledon, and American) in one year, 1938. When he accomplished this, the feat was not viewed with the same awe we attach to it today (partly because fewer players then made the trip to play in Australia), but it marked a new high point in tennis.

Born in Oakland, California in 1916, Budge had sport in his blood: his father had played football for the Scottish team Glasgow Rangers. He preferred basketball, neighborhood football and baseball to tennis in his youth. But in 1930 his older brother Hugh taunted him into entering the California State Boy's Tennis Tournament, and after practising furiously in secret, he turned up and won it.

The redheaded teenager worked hard to perfect every stroke in the book. Two years later he won the Pacific Coast junior tournament, and in 1933 gained the junior and senior singles titles of California. The following year the tall thin all rounder was spotted by Walter Pate, who picked him for his 1935 Davis Cup team. In a preliminary round Budge was pitched in against the world number two, Australia's Jack Crawford. They battled for four hours 10 minutes, and Budge astonished the tennis world by winning the match. Exhausted, he began suffering terrible cramps, and Crawford passed out completely.

Fred Perry dominated tennis at this time, and Budge studied him as much as possible, learning to play with similar sustained aggression, and to move in quickly to the net after a forcing shot. Budge now had an excellent all round game: powerful service, strong groundstrokes, blistering forehand, and a deadly topspin backhand drive which dealt particularly well with service returns. In addition, he was a fluid mover, had good concentration, and despite his red hair, an even, controled temperament.

In 1936 he met Perry in the US Final, and held two match points against the Englishman before succumbing. When Perry went professional, Budge had the chance to establish himself at the top. At the next Wimbledon, he became the first player to achieve the triple crown, beating von Cramm in the singles, and teaming up with Gene Mako and Alice Marble for his doubles titles. He also met von Cramm that year in a marathon Davis Cup match. Von Cramm had been encouraged by a phone call from the Führer himself before the match, and took the first two sets. Budge fought back for the next two, but went down 1-4 in the fifth. Leveling once again, he missed

ABOVE: Don Budge was highly competitive, having learned both sustained aggression and the importance of refreshment from Fred Perry.

ABOVE RIGHT: Budge watches doubles partner Gene Mako smash a winner. They won two doubles titles at both Wimbledon and Forest Hills.

BOTTOM RIGHT: Britain's Bunny Austin congratulates Budge after his 1938 victory at Wimbledon.

BOTTOM LEFT: Budge on his way to his 1932 US title win. His best stroke was a vicious topspin backhand.

five match points before scrambling back a German cross court forehand as he fell for the winner. The story illustrates Budge's determination to fight for every point on the tennis court.

1938 was Budge's year. In Australia, he beat John Bromwich for the title, going on to defeat Czechoslovakian Roderick Menzel in the French – both wins in straight sets. Reaching the Wimbledon final, he faced Britain's Bunny Austin, eagerly supported by the patriotic crowd, but only lost four games in taking the title. Just for good measure, he achieved a second Wimbledon triple crown that year, with the same partners as in 1937. Now everything hinged on the US championships, where he faced his doubles partner Gene Mako, but he overpowered him 6-3, 6-8, 6-2, 6-1. He had won every Grand Slam title of the year. No-one would repeat the feat until Rod Laver in 1962.

Budge turned professional after that, and proved more than a match for Vines, Perry and Tilden on the professional circuit. To many people, he was the complete tennis player, matching superb skills with an equable temperament.

PART III
Raising the Profile
1946-1967

The victorious Wightman Cup team of 1966. Billie Jean King is third from left, and on her left is Nancy Richey. Far right is captain and former star Doris Hart.

The Path to Professionalism

LEFT: *Jack Kramer sends up a lob against Pancho Gonzales during Gonzales' first professional game. Kramer beat him 6-4, 3-6, 6-3, 6-2.*

BELOW: *Kramer and Gonzales after the match, watched by 13,357 spectators.*

RIGHT: *Billie Jean King celebrating a win over Margaret Court on Wimbledon Centre Court in 1962.*

Tennis between 1946 and 1968 was a changing game. The number of top male players cast out from the amateur world because they chose to turn professional became an absurd, counterproductive drain on all the major championships. The game was divided into two worlds, one populated by maverick professionals, the other by establishment amateurs – who were paid under the table. The length of time tennis took to rectify this nonsense is an indictment of its officials over a number of years.

The path to professionalism was pioneered to a great extent by Jack Kramer. During the 1950s he lured just about every player who won the US and Wimbledon titles on to his professional tours, which genuinely pitched the best tennis talent together night after grueling night, in the most unlikely settings – ice rinks, football stadiums, gymnasiums: anywhere a court could be set up.

Meanwhile the amateurs lined up in hotels for their 'expenses', or found their tennis shoes stuffed with appearance money cash. Many players traveled with sports bags bulging not with equipment, but bank notes. They would plan their year's schedule in a series of encounters in the players' tea room at Wimbledon during the championships – because everybody of any import in the game was there to negotiate with.

All but the crustiest residents of amateur officialdom accepted that it was in the interests of tennis to unite the two groupings. In 1960 the ILTF narrowly voted down a motion to implement some form of professional tennis, depriving the major tournaments of talent such as Pancho Gonzales, Alex Olmedo, Lew Hoad and Ken Rosewall.

In 1967 when more than 300,000 spectators set a record attendance at Wimbledon, Herman David, of the All England Club, shocked the ILTF by announcing that next year's tournament would be 'open', accepting entries from professionals. Wimbledon was the citadal of world tennis, and for all its powers and threats, there was little the ILTF could actually do to stop the move.

In fact the first Open tournament in tennis was organized by the British LTA for BBC television, and held in May 1968, at Bournemouth on England's south coast. Britain's Mark Cox became the first amateur to beat a professional in an authorized tournament, winning over Pancho Gonzales. Ken Rosewall defeated Rod Laver in the final, and Virginia Wade became the first woman open champion when she beat Winnie Shaw. It was the end of an era of absurdity, and the beginning of modern tennis.

Another post war trend was the Australian challenge to America's dominance; many American players turned professional and they were replaced by a succession of skilled Australians, many trained by Harry Hopman. The women's game was unaffected by professionalism, and here Great Britain was replaced by Australia for the place alongside America as the pair of leading nations.

LEFT: *Ken Rosewall, whose career spanned two decades. He was shy and disciplined, unlike his fellow 'magic twin' Lew Hoad.*

RIGHT: *The impressive and impulsive Lew Hoad at the height of his career.*

BELOW: *Tony Trabert, who won the Wimbledon title in 1955 without dropping a set – as he did in 1953 and 1955 at Forest Hills.*

In 1963, to celebrate its 50th anniversary, the ILTF donated a trophy for an international women's team competition, the Federation Cup. The large silver flower bowl was to be the women's equivalent of the Davis Cup, except it would be fought for during a one week team knock out tournament, each tie consisting of two singles and one doubles match. Sixteen nations contested the first Federation Cup in London the week before Wimbledon in June 1963. America met Australia in the final, and with Margaret Court beating Darlene Hard, and Billie Jean Moffitt winning over Lesley Turner, it all hinged on the doubles. The American pair clinched it 3-6, 13-11, 6-3.

These two countries fought the first three finals, but West Germany beat Australia on Italian clay in 1966, to earn a place in the finals against America, and Great Britain reached (and lost) the finals the next year.

The 1968 Federation Cup venue was Paris – in the middle of the student riots – and the dramatic events outside the stadium were matched inside as the unseeded Dutch team got to the final, where they lost to Australia. Although now attracting an entry of 23 teams, the Cup was not yet established as a major tennis event, and its instigation is evidence of a growing interest in women's tennis, which was later to accelerate rapidly.

The major championships at Wimbledon, the USA and Australia are described in separate chapters, but the French tournament should also be noted as it helped to establish some major clay court specialists, such as Italy's Nicola Pietrangeli, or the Czech refugee Jaroslav Drobny, who both won the title twice. In 1961 Pietrangeli was trying for his third succesive French title, facing Spain's Manuel Santana. The match went to five exciting sets, and ended with the victorious Spaniard weeping on the shoulder of his disappointed opponent.

French success in their own tournament was limited – Marcel Bernard recovered from a two set deficit against Drobny to take the men's title in 1946, and Nelly Landry (British born, French by marriage) won in 1948, but it was 1967 before Françoise Durr delighted the home crowd with her 4-6, 6-3, 6-4 victory over Lesley Turner.

Wimbledon Back in Business

Wimbledon was back in business in 1946, bomb damaged and short of decent food – rationing was still in operation and most players from abroad brought their own supplies.

Over the next 20 years, America and Australia battled for top spot virtually unchallenged – between them they took the men's singles title 18 times. This was particularly remarkable because they kept having to produce new talent for the challenge; the professional game was growing and many champions opted to turn pro immediately after gaining a Wimbledon title. The championships of 1948, 1953, 1956, 1958, 1959,1960 and 1963 did not feature the title holder. In common with all other major tournaments, Wimbledon only accepted amateur players (however false that claim of amateurism was). By the 1960s some argued that Wimbledon was offering second class tennis, and the tournament eventually went open in 1968.

In 1946 the title favorites were the American Jack Kramer, and Australian Dinny Pails. But Kramer lost in the fourth round with a badly blistered hand, and Pails got lost on the London Underground

system, arriving late and flustered for his match with Frenchman Yvon Petra, and was beaten. Petra went on to win the title.

Kramer had some compensation winning the doubles with Tom Brown, and met his doubles partner in the 1947 final, having cantered through the earlier rounds. He emerged the winner in just 48 minutes. The win began a long sequence of American victories in the men's singles, with Californian Bob Falkenburg in 1948 probably the least popular winner ever, because of his slow movements between points to conserve his energies. This often led him to give up games and even sets so that he was fresh for the key moments in the match. He did stir himself to save three championship points, though. Another Californian, stocky Ted Schroeder, won the 1949 final, outserving Czech Jaroslav Drobny in a tense five-setter.

In 1950 rain stopped play, not for the first or last time at Wimbledon, but the crowd reacted angrily and chanted for their money back. They were placated with priority admission for the next day, in a year when the American winners were in fact surprise victors. Budge Patty lived in Paris, and had a more European playing style with an array of elegant passing shots and forehand drives. He had already won the French championships, and defeated Australia's Frank Sedgman to win the Wimbledon title. Then in 1951 Dick Savitt from New Jersey got through to the final at his first attempt, and easily beat another Australian, Ken McGregor, as he had done in the Australian championships.

1952 saw the Wimbledon debuts of the great Australians Lew Hoad and Ken Rosewall, but it was their compatriot Frank Sedgman who finally won the Wimbledon title and broke the American stranglehold on the men's championship. He was the first Australian men's champion since Jack Crawford in 1933.

The 1953 championship will always be remembered for a marathon match of over four hours between Budge Patty and Jaroslav Drobny. They were close friends and knew each other's game inside out. Starting at 5.00pm, and finishing in the eerie dusk past 9.00pm, they fought a total of 93 games and Drobny saved six match points on his way to victory. The Czech Drobny was a tremendously popular champion the next year, partly because he had ended his nomadic years by marrying an Englishwoman and settling in Sussex. In beating the 19-year-old Ken Rosewall (14 years his junior) in a match of superb tennis, and the longest in Wimbledon history at

ABOVE: *Both Trabert and Rex Hartwig were successful in 1955. Hartwig (right) teamed up with fellow Australian Lew Hoad to retain his doubles title.*

LEFT: *Wimbledon champion of 1952, Frank Sedgman leaps for a volley. He won the US title in the same year.*

LEFT: *Gorgeous Gussy Moran's famous lace panties, viewed with delight by the press, and with dismay by the authorities.*

BELOW: *Louise Brough (right) and Maureen Connolly in action, 1952.*

58 games, Drobny became the first left-handed title winner since Norman Brookes in 1907.

America's Tony Trabbert won 21 sets on the trot in 1955 to take the title in a year when he won the French and US championships and reached the semi-final of the Australian tournament. He turned professional the same year, a further illustration of how Wimbledon and other championships were diminished by their insistence on the amateur status of entrants.

Lew Hoad clasped the winner's trophy for the following two years, turning professional the day after he retained his title. Fellow Australian Rod Laver, probably the greatest player in the history of the game, was losing finalist for two years running before gaining the title in 1961, and retaining it the next year. But Australia continued to produce Wimbledon champions, benefiting from the groundwork done by Harry Hopman during the 1950s in developing young talent. Roy Emerson won two titles and John Newcombe one, as the men's title repeatedly went down under in the mid-1960s.

The years 1946 to 1967 were not as eventful in the women's game, where professionalism had not really established itself. But in 1949 a sensation put women's tennis on the front pages of all the papers, although the game itself was quite overshadowed. Gussy Moran, a beautiful 25-year-old, appeared on court wearing, under her ballerina skirt, a pair of pink lace panties designed by Ted Tinling. At a time when post war shortages had made ladieswear rather drab, the interest in these innocuous garments was intense. The All England Club felt they lacked decorum, and Tinling left after 35 years' service. 'Georgous Gussy', as she was known, reached the ladies doubles final.

America was supreme in women's tennis, producing an astonishing array of truly exceptional players. American women won the singles title 13 times from 1946, and ten consecutive years in

ABOVE LEFT: *A great rival of Margaret Court, and a major star of the late 1950s and 1960s, the graceful Maria Bueno.*

BELOW LEFT: *The 1947 US Wightman Cup team trounced Britain 7-0. Left to right – Hazel Wightman, Patricia Canning Todd, Doris Hart, Margaret Osborne (Du Pont), Louise Brough and Shirley Fry.*

RIGHT: *The first black title holder at Wimbledon was the talented Althea Gibson in 1957, seen here with defeated finalist, Darlene Hard.*

the doubles. Four of these singles titles went to Louise Brough from Oklahoma, who echoed Alice Marble in her aggressive serve and volley tactics. Tall and blond, she was triple Wimbledon champion in 1948 and 1950, partnered in the women's doubles by Margaret DuPont (née Osborne) with whom she formed a truly formidable pairing. She would have been triple champion in 1949 too, had she and John Bromwich not lost the mixed doubles final on a day when Brough played three finals, spending five hours 20 minutes on court and playing eight sets of tennis.

1951 saw another triple crown, achieved this time by Doris Hart of St Louis, Missouri. Highly mobile despite a leg withered by polio, she possessed superb serve and touch shots, and won five successive mixed doubles titles at Wimbledon. Louise Brough's dominance at Wimbledon was further interrupted by Maureen Connolly, who would surely have won many more titles than her three consecutive wins from 1952 to 1954 had her career not been cut short by a riding accident.

However, Brough won again in 1955, and American dominance continued with wins by Shirley Fry and two by Althea Gibson, the

first black top tennis player. From a tough Harlem background, Althea Gibson had a fierce service and excellent strength and reach. She won her first Wimbledon title in 1957 aged 29, receiving the trophy from the Queen, and retaining her title the next year.

In 1958 Althea Gibson also won the doubles, partnered by a future Wimbledon legend and champion, Maria Bueno. Born in Sao Paulo, Brazil, Maria Bueno played with grace and artistry hindered only by her sometimes wayward concentration – rather like Evonne Goolagong was to be. She and Margaret Court were the major women's tennis players of their day, and had many memorable battles including the 1964 Wimbledon final. Bueno captured her first Wimbledon singles in 1959, and was to win the title three times in five finals. She used to study her opponents' games carefully and adjust her balletic, all court game to suit it. After winning two consecutive titles, jaundice forced her out of competition in 1961, and in 1962 she lost to the unseeded Vera Sukova. She made a dramatic comeback in 1964, beating Margaret Court (then Margaret Smith) in the final. She lost to the Australian in the final the next year, and the year after to Billie Jean King. She also won five doubles titles.

America Invaded

In the postwar years, Americans struggled to win their own national championship against a string of powerful players now better able to roam the globe looking for glory. The Australians in particular, seemed to feel that the US title was theirs by right. American interest in tennis reached a new peak, and for the first time since 1937, the gates of Forest Hills had to be closed to limit the attendance. In nine days 62,509 spectators came to the singles championships, despite the first ever TV coverage by NBC.

America dominated the women's game (untainted by professionalism) after the Second World War. Superb players, such as Louise Brough, Margaret DuPont (who together formed the top doubles team), Doris Hart and Pauline Betz, swept all before them.

Margaret DuPont, from Oregon, commenced a run of three US singles titles in 1948, with a 4-6, 6-4, 15-13 win over Louise Brough, who had already won the first of her three successive Wimbledon titles. In 1950, on the way to her third title, Mrs DuPont beat Althea Gibson, the first black player to appear on Center Court at Forest Hills. Mrs DuPont captured her eighth successive doubles title that year, too (all won with Louise Brough) and together they took another three US doubles titles later in the decade.

The story of Maureen Connolly's short, brilliant tennis career which included the next three US titles is told later, and her successor as champion was the plucky Doris Hart.

For four years from 1956, the US women's champion was the current Wimbledon title holder: Shirley Fry, Althea Gibson (twice), and Maria Bueno all achieved the feat, and by 1960 Maria Bueno, as Wimbledon queen, was expected to repeat the achievement. She

ABOVE: *Doris Hart was an excellent player despite the handicap of a weak leg. Here she is congratulated by Britain's Mrs Rinkel after a Wightman Cup match.*

RIGHT: *Calm, collected Maureen Connolly faces up to the forceful Doris Hart in their 1951 US semi-final. Aged only 16, Connolly won, and went on to beat Shirley Fry in the final.*

ABOVE FAR RIGHT: *Roy Emerson slashes a return to Rod Laver in the 1962 US national. Laver went on to win the title and became the second man to win a Grand Slam.*

BELOW RIGHT: *Frank Sedgman on his way to his second US title in 1952. He reaches to return a shot from Tony Trabert, who he beat to reach the quarter finals.*

reached the US finals to meet the aggressive volleyer Darlene Hard, her doubles partner that year, but lost 6-4, 10-12, 6-4.

History was made that year when Mrs DuPont won her third successive mixed doubles title with Neale Fraser, bringing her total of US national championship titles to a record 25.

While the American women ruled tennis through the 1950s, it was Australians who dominated in the men's arena, as American champions such as Kramer, winner in 1946 and 1947, and the great Gonzales, who won in 1948 and 1949, went professional and out of the mainstream game. An illustrious line of Australians, beginning with Frank Sedgman and including Ken Rosewall, Neale Fraser, Roy Emerson and Rod Laver, took nine out of 12 US singles championships between 1951 and 1962. Only Tony Trabbert (twice) and Vic Seixas of America could break the Australian grip on the championship during these years.

One of the gutsiest of those Australian wins was by Ashley Cooper, who injured his ankle in the 12th game of the fifth set of his 1958 final against fellow Australian, top seeded Mal Anderson. Cooper fought on to win the title 6-2, 3-6, 4-6, 10-8, 8-6, leaving him only one title (the French) short of a Grand Slam.

The run of Australian title wins was broken not by America but Mexico, whose Rafael Osuna showed his delicate touch in beating the USA's Frank Froehling in 1963. For the next four years, all the men's singles titles went down under (apart from a win by the Spanish topspin specialist Manuel Santana in 1965). By 1967, the Americans had not won their own national men's title for 12 years.

In the 1960s, the women's title started going abroad too, with Maria Bueno and Australia's Margaret Smith (later Court) winning the finals from 1962 until 1967. This was despite the strength of the American women's game, shown by their success in the Federation Cup, an international team championship for women. America won in the inaugural year 1963, and again in 1966 and 1967, when Billie Jean King clinched her first US singles title. The year was significant, for it marked the final amateur national singles contest at Forest Hills: the professional era had arrived at last.

Hopman's Miracle Kids

In the 1950s, Australia suddenly stamped its personality on world tennis, producing a string of great male players who individually took major titles around the globe, and collectively won and retained the Davis Cup many times.

The architect of much of this success was Harry Hopman. An excellent tennis player in his day, Hopman became a journalist, and used his free time and energy – he and his wife Nell had no children – to become trainer and coach to young Australian tennis talent. Hopman helped to shape some of the top sportsmen of the 1950s and 1960s: Sedgman, Hoad, Rosewall, Emerson, Fraser, Laver, Newcombe and Roche. If ever a country produced a group of players to rival the skills and spirit of France's Four Musketeers, it was Hopman's 'Miracle Kids'. Their triumphs were his victories. He was Australia's Davis Cup captain from 1950 to 1969, during which time his teams won the trophy on 15 occasions.

'The Fox', as he was known, was a strict disciplinarian, 'fining' pupils for misdemeanours with punishingly long runs. Applying the principles of sports training to Kramer's aggressive 'Big Game', players began to spend as much time in the gym as on the courts, building up strength and stamina as well as tennis technique and an understanding of match strategy. He was able to capitalize on the strong interest in tennis in the country, the sunny climate which allows virtually year round play, and the use of a surface – grass – which encourages hard hitting and quick thinking. He also benefited from a highly organized tennis establishment which ran good tournaments and did all it could to dissuade players from turning professional. Shamateurism was rife in Australian tennis throughout this period. All the major players had so-called 'jobs' with sports manu-

facturers, and many were given extra benefits as financial incentives – one became the owner of a petrol station! Finally, Hopman inherited a doubles playing culture: doubles was regarded as excellent practice and training, and fostered a powerful team spirit. Australian pairings such as Quist and Bromwich (who together won the Australian doubles title eight times from 1938 to 1950) gave the doubles game credibility, and players from down under have traditionally been superb doubles performers.

Frank Sedgman was the first of Hopman's great champions, an intuitive, quick, player with a superb forehand. Teamed with Ken McGregor he did the doubles Grand Slam in 1951, the year he also became the first Australian to win the US nationals. He never lost a Davis Cup doubles match, and picked up all the major singles titles except France before turning pro in 1953.

As Sedgman turned pro, Hopman was bringing on his next couple of protegés, two young men born 21 days apart, who were opposites in playing style and character: Lew Hoad and Ken Rosewall. Dubbed 'the magic twins', these 19-year-olds together helped retain the Davis Cup in 1953. One of the key matches involved Lew Hoad. Pitched against America's Tony Trabert, Hoad took 90 minutes to win the first set 13-11, but lost the next two. 0-30 down at 5-5 in the fourth, the teenager looked on his way out, but he thrived on big match pressure and won the next two games to take the match.

Hoad was powerfully built, a serve and volley man with a vicious topspin backhand. Rosewall was small (earning him the sarcastic nickname 'muscles'), a superb strokemaker, graceful and economical. While Hoad was rash and impulsive, Rosewall was quiet and serious. They complemented each other so well that in 1953 they won the Wimbledon, Australian and French doubles titles. Three years later Hoad looked set for a Grand Slam, winning in Australia, Paris and Wimbledon, but met his partner Rosewall in the US nationals, and lost in four sets. They took the doubles title together. Hoad took the Wimbledon singles again in 1957 with a crushing 57-minute win over Ashley Cooper. He then turned pro, but back trouble ended his career prematurely.

In contrast Rosewall just kept going, in a career which spanned 25

ABOVE LEFT: *Harry Hopman cultivated Australia's postwar tennis talent.*

BELOW LEFT: *The 1962 Davis Cup victors after trouncing Mexico 5-0. From left Roy Emerson, Ken Fletcher, Rod Laver, Neale Fraser and Harry Hopman.*

ABOVE: *Frank Sedgman was the first Australian to win the Wimbledon men's singles since the war. Here he receives his trophy from the Duchess of Kent.*

BELOW: *One match away from a Grand Slam, Lew Hoad rises to smash a Rosewall lob at the 1956 US final. Rosewall outlasted his compatriot to win the match.*

RIGHT: *Roy Emerson was a notable schoolboy athlete – at 14 he ran the 100 yards in 10.6 seconds. His speed, agility and power made him a formidable tennis player.*

BELOW RIGHT: *An all-Australian doubles semi-final at Wimbledon in 1961. Roy Emerson goes for a volley watched by partner Neale Fraser. This side of the net are Ken Fletcher and John Newcombe, who lost the match. The Australians use doubles play as practice and for team building.*

ABOVE: *Forest Hills 1974, and Rosewall is not a match for Connors, who clobbered the veteran Australian in one hour, eight minutes.*

RIGHT: *Lew Hoad lands on his back during the 1957 Wimbledon, and watches the ball that eluded him roll on. He didn't take it lying down, though, and managed to retain the title.*

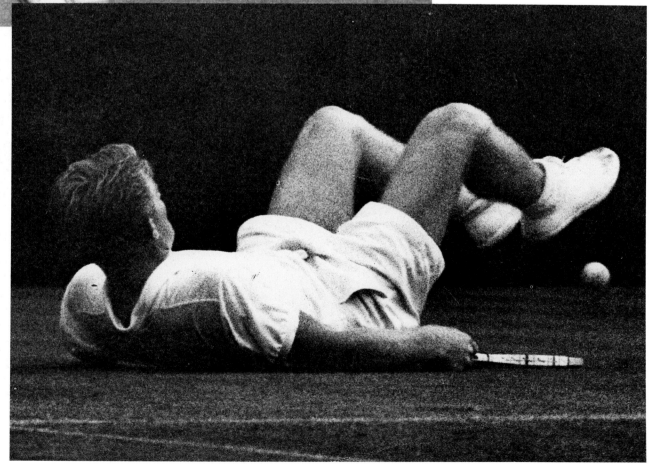

years, during which he won every major title except the Wimbledon singles. He played with a rare finesse and delicacy, racing across the court to flick shots back despite his frail appearance. Naturally left handed, he was taught to play with his other hand, which slightly weakened his service action. By the time he turned professional in 1956, he had collected singles and doubles title in the USA and France once each, plus two Wimbledon doubles titles, and the Australian singles championship twice, notching up two doubles wins with his friend and rival Lew Hoad. As a pro, Rosewall was the world champion from 1960 to 1965, and in the Open tennis era he picked up the French title in 1968, 15 years after he had first won it. In later years he won one US Open and the Australian title twice. In 1974 he faced Jimmy Connors in the Wimbledon and US finals, but was blasted off the court, in a sorry end to an amazing career.

Another of Hopman's prodigies, Roy Emerson, filled the gap after Laver had turned pro. He is not remembered as often as many of his contemporaries, but won more major titles than anyone else in tennis – 32 in all – partly because he stayed an amateur. Fast on his feet, with strong wrists (developed from milking cows in Blackheat, Queensland), he was rigorously trained by Hopman to turn out a fearsome serve and solid groundstrokes and volleys. Emerson led Australia's Davis Cup challenge in the early 1960s, and picked up six Australian, two Wimbledon, two US and two French singles titles. He also led a revolt by the players against the all powerful Australian tennis establishment which only allowed them to play abroad for 210 days per year. He finally turned pro in 1968, just before Open tennis arrived.

Emerson's contemporary and early doubles partner Neale Fraser remained an amateur, and had a distinguished career which ended after he reached the Wimbledon doubles final at the age of 40 in 1973. A copybook serve and volleyer, Fraser beat Laver in the 1960 Wimbledon final, the year he retained his US title. Ironically for someone who served his country for many years in the Davis Cup, he never won his own national title.

The Australian men ruled the tennis world, and by the close of the 1960s, the Australian women were on their way to establishing a similar position in their game. The women's game in Australia was fairly quiet until the arrival of the great Margaret Court, and her successes encouraged the Australian women to win the Federation Cup three times during the 1960s in 1964, 1965, and 1968.

The Davis Cup Boomerang

Dwight Davis died in November 1945, leaving behind him a permanent reminder of his wish to bring sporting unity to the tennis world. In his career as a diplomat he sometimes found his past role in starting the Davis Cup a little cumbersome – people were more interested in talking about the famous competition than exchanging diplomatic niceties. But tennis always had a special place in his life. In 1930, while based in the Philippines, he wrote that he still played the game. 'I find that most of the vim, vigour and vitality has disappeared but manage to hobble around the court fairly well and occasionally get a ball back. It has been the best way of getting exercise and has been a lifesaver for me.'

The emerging giant of the game in the postwar years was Jack Kramer, who proved himself a tough negotiator amidst the internal politics of the American camp. There were arguments over expenses, whether wives could travel with the team, selection, and other issues, none of them conducive to team spirit.

In 1946 America visited Australia as the underdogs in the Davis Cup challenge round, and the attacking style of Kramer, and the ruthless serve and volleyer Ted Schroeder, won a famous victory. The loss had a tremendous impact on Australian tennis for they realized they had faced a new breed of athlete in the contest. Players spent more and more time in the gymnasium as they aimed for more speed and strength, harangued by the disciplinarian coach and captain Harry Hopman. The lesson was well learned by the new generation of players, for from 1950 to 1967 Australia won the Davis Cup on all occasions but three, when the Americans stopped the trophy returning down under like a boomerang.

In 1950, Australian fitness and intelligent play won back the cup, with McGregor exploiting Schroeder's weak passing strokes, a chink in his armor that Hopman had detected as the American warmed up on a separate court just before the match.

Twelve months later, 40 years after the last challenge round held in Sydney, temporary stands at White City accommodated 15,300 spectators for a contest with the USA which truly caught the Australian public imagination.

Frank Sedgman was the Australian hero, and Harry Hopman gave careful advice to his protegé in the final deciding match against Victor Seixas in 1951. Hopman advised him to play soft volleys at the feet of his opponent rather than try to hit winners, as this would confuse the American. Hopman knew that Sedgman was capable of switching tactics quickly because he was so proficient in his whole game. The Australian won in straight sets.

The same result emerged between these two men the following year, as Australia again defeated the USA, but the night after the win, Sedgman and McGregor announced that they had decided to turn professional. Australia filled the gap with Lew Hoad and Ken Rosewall, the 'magic twins' from Sydney.

In 1953 they faced the Americans in a thrilling contest. Rosewall played so poorly in his first singles that he was replaced as Lew Hoad's partner in the doubles by Rex Hartwig. Hartwig learned he was to play at two hours notice, as he was about to catch a tram home. The switch was an imaginative move, but it failed because Hoad and Hartwig had not played doubles together often enough to gel as a team.

RIGHT: *Frank Sedgman, who never lost a Davis Cup doubles match.*

ABOVE FAR RIGHT: *The American and Australian 1950 Challenge Round teams. Left to right: Australians George Worthington, John Bromwich, Ken McGregor, Frank Sedgman and William Talbert; and Americans Ted Schroeder, Tom Brown, and Gardner Mulloy.*

BELOW FAR RIGHT: *Hopman's training sessions were infamous. A minor transgression was penalized with a long punishment run. (Left to right): John Bromwich, George Worthington, Mervyn Rose, Frank Sedgman, Ken McGregor, and Harry Hopman.*

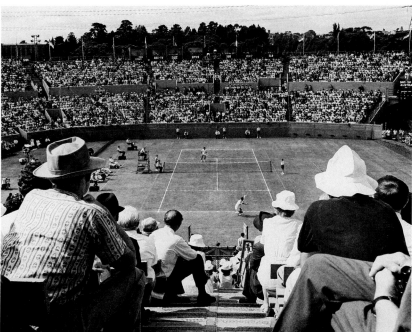

The Australians were also perplexed by the Americans Victor Seixas and Tony Trabert's 'scissor' system, developed a few years before. When the Americans had serve, the man at the net would face his partner and signal where he would move as soon as the service was made. This meant that the Australians saw the server and the back of his partner, and could only guess the likely positions of their opponents for the service return. Hopman felt this practice was pretty poor sportsmanship as it held the game up.

The next tie was a long encounter between Hoad and Trabert played in damp conditions which forced Hoad to wear spikes, which he was unused to, and then to change rackets after his favored one broke. This was fortuitous as the dry and tight replacement helped his game. Hoad emerged the winner and when Rosewall beat Seixas the next day, all Australia celebrated another great victory. The following year Seixas and Trabert gained revenge by defeating the Sydney twins to take the cup back to the States but in 1955 back came the cup to Australia as America suffered its worst defeat in a challenge round since Great Britain had trounced her in 1935.

Australia was winning the Davis Cup consistently, but there was a surprise in 1960: they still won, but it was the Italians who had battled through the zonal contests to fight it out. Guided by Jaroslav Drobny, the Italian team sensationally beat the Americans in Perth, and for the first time since 1936, America failed to reach the challenge round of the Davis Cup. It was a result that provided a major boost to the minor tennis nations, and the drubbing the Italians received from the holders in the challenge round did not lessen the impact of their achievement.

After the Italians repeated the feat in 1961, the big shock the next year was the arrival of Mexico in the challenge round to meet Australia. The Mexicans had beaten America in Mexico City and gone on to win the American zone. On the grass of Brisbane, the Mexicans were less formidable, and lost all five ties to a team which included Rod Laver.

After the USA and Australia had shared the honors for two years, the small fry came back into the frame in 1965 when Spain reached the final hurdle. She won only one match. The next year India, and Spain again in 1967, suffered similar losses against the formidable Australians. Soon, however, Emerson, Newcombe and Roche were to turn professional, much to the relief of the other 40 or so nations who were now regularly entering the contest.

TOP LEFT: *Ken Rosewall on his way to his first Wimbledon final, after beating Tony Trabert in 1954. He lost the match 13-11, 4-6, 6-2, 9-7 to Jaroslav Drobny.*

ABOVE LEFT: *The scene as Australia beat India 4-1 to retain the Davis Cup in 1966.*

LEFT: *Rex Hartwig, another of Hopman's protegés.*

RIGHT: *Maureen Connolly poses for a 22nd birthday shot, by which time she had already achieved her Grand Slam.*

Little Mo

Maureen Connolly – 'Little Mo' – was the first woman to win the Grand Slam, and was on the path to legendary status when her tennis playing career was ended by a horse riding accident. There is a great deal of evidence to suggest that she would have become the greatest woman player of all time. She was US champion on her first attempt at the age of 16, and kept the title for three years. She also won Wimbledon on her first visit in 1952, and retained that title for three years, too.

Connolly was brought up in San Diego and as a child, she peered through a fence one day, fascinated by the sight of a tennis professional, Wilbur Folsom, showing off a few of his strokes. They met, and he spotted her determination to win and became her first coach, charging Mrs Connolly 50 cents instead of his usual $25 per hour. He persuaded his pupil to switch from her left-handed grip, and tutored her in match tactics and stroke play.

Moving on to the famous coach Eleanor Tennant, Connolly perfected a fast, accurate, baseline game which allowed her the luxury of hardly ever having to volley – at least not under pressure – as she played her attacking groundstrokes so near the lines. At the age of 14 Connolly became the youngest girl ever to win the national junior championships. By 1951 she was ranked third in the world, having defeated her childhood heroine Doris Hart in the semi final of the US Championships, and then beat Shirley Fry in the final, urged on by the formidable 'Teach' Tennant. She was the youngest player to win the title for nearly 50 years.

'Little Mo' was ruthless and single minded. She learned to psyche herself up for her matches, and marked each winning point with a vigorous nod, a gesture indicating her mental aggression. On court, she worked up an emotionally draining hatred for her opponent. She believed people would only like her if she carried on winning, and 'Little Mo' wanted to be liked.

Training in England for Wimbledon in 1952, she shocked observers by slugging out practice games with men for sessions of more than four hours. No woman player had shown this intensity before. Indeed, her coach had advised her to pull out as she was carrying an injury, but she insisted on playing, and broke her relationship with Eleanor Tennant. That first year at Wimbledon, in the fourth round, as Connolly faced match point against Susan Partridge, an encouraging shout from an American in the crowd inspired her to victory. The set she dropped in that match and another in the quarter final were the only two she ever lost at Wimbledon. Reaching the final, she beat Louise Brough in straight sets.

Her 8-6, 7-5 victory over Hart in the Wimbledon final in 1953 was considered one of the finest women's matches ever played.
That year saw her achieve the first ever Grand Slam by a woman, winning the Australian, French, US and Wimbledon titles – and in all of them, except the Australian, it was Hart she beat in the finals.

In July 1954, fresh from another Wimbledon triumph, and an argument with her lover, she went out riding. Her horse bolted straight into a lorry that had startled it, crushing Maureen's right leg. Not yet 20, her career was over, despite some attempts at a comeback. It was a tragedy for a spirited and talented sportswoman who

ABOVE: *Connolly stoops to conquer Doris Hart for the second year running in the US singles final.*

ABOVE FAR RIGHT: *Eleanor 'Teach' Tennant ensures her pupil Maureen Connolly is wrapped up against the cold. They fell out when the famous coach tried to stop the injured Connolly playing at Wimbledon. Ruthless Little Mo ditched her coach, but won the title.*

BELOW FAR RIGHT: *Little Mo with her third successive Wimbledon trophy in 1954.*

MIDDLE: *Little Mo in 1951. The smile conceals ruthless determination.*

RIGHT: *On the way to her 1952 finals win over Louise Brough.*

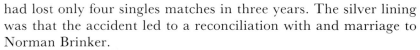

had lost only four singles matches in three years. The silver lining was that the accident led to a reconciliation with and marriage to Norman Brinker.

'Little Mo' died from cancer, aged 34, in 1969. She was a fiercely competitive player who would have taken major titles for many years. Perhaps because of the hatred she summoned up on the tennis court, she did not achieve much in doubles play. She is commemorated by the Maureen Connolly Trophy, contested by young players from Britain and the US every fall.

Kramer vs. the Establishment

RIGHT: *Jack Kramer checks his palm. Hand blisters cost him a Wimbledon title in 1946 . . .*

ABOVE RIGHT: *. . . but the all-American boy was back the next year to sweep up the trophy.*

BELOW RIGHT: *Kramer is congratulated by C. Spychalla of Poland after an easy victory early in the 1947 Wimbledon tournament.*

Jack Kramer did more to shape the modern game of tennis than any other man. A tennis champion in his own right, throughout the 1950s and early 1960s he organized the professional game into a proper circuit, signing up just about every major player, and bringing to it a new credibility, as well as popular appeal. Without him, the arrival of Open tennis would probably have been delayed even longer.

Kramer took a professional attitude to the way he played tennis as an amateur, following the rules of percentage play which had been devised by an engineer called Cliff Roche. Rule one was: always hold your serve; rule two: only attack your opponent's serve when the score is 0-30. There were various complex calculations of the best placement of shots against say, left-handers, or good volleyers, but the basic concept of percentage tennis was to prioritize the points, and only go all out for the important ones. That way, you pace yourself properly to last the game, and when you have opportunities, you

are not too tired to capitalize on them.

A keen sportsman, Kramer saw an exhibition match between Vines and Tilden in 1935 at the age of 14, and was captivated by the glamorous, majestic Vines. The next year he won the National Boys Singles and Doubles titles unseeded, in a field which included Bobby Riggs and Ted Schroeder. By 1938 he was ranked 15th in America, and was developing his 'Big Game' – powerful serves and quick volleys, supported by an extremely accurate, placed but not forced, forehand drive. He was not a natural player, but his application and shrewdness made him a winner. The following year he was the youngest player ever to participate in the Davis Cup – a record which held until 1968. His career was interrupted by illness and war service, but he won the US National doubles title with Ted Schroeder in 1940 and 1941, and in 1943 with Frank Parker. Favorite to win Wimbledon in 1946, a badly blistered hand contributed to his

fourth round defeat by Drobny. The calculating Kramer devised a game plan for the next year: he would win the US and Wimbledon titles and turn pro.

Sure enough, at Wimbledon he easily won the title, dropping only one set in the championship (against Dinny Pails, who said 'he missed everything by a hair for a quarter of an hour'). Kramer won the final against Tom Brown – who he had beaten for the US singles title the previous year – in 45 ruthless minutes. Expecting to face Frank Parker in the US final, Kramer brought in a coach to improve his cross court forehand, a vital stroke against his opponent. It worked, although he went two sets down before overrunning his opponent 4-6, 2-6, 6-1, 6-0, 6-3. Kramer was never afraid to learn from others – he copied Perry and Schroeder in their choice of sweet tea as on-court refreshment instead of carbonated drinks, for example.

As a pro he trounced Bobby Riggs 69-20 on their tour, learning to get to the net early against the wily ex-champion. He won the US Pro championship in 1948, and later beat Pancho Gonzales 96-27 on their tour: he was unquestionably the best tennis talent of the 1940s.

Kramer saw there was more money to be made in promoting, and he fed the growing interest in the professional game by signing up a succession of amateur champions to play the established pros. Cast out by the amateur establishment, the professional circuit played at any venue it could, and threatened to turn the amateur game into second class fare. He felt that the amateur game would be more prepared to change its rules to allow the professionals back without him as a figurehead, Kramer stepped out of the limelight in 1962, but remained involved with the game and helped to devise the World Championship Tennis format in later years.

Gonzales the Lion

The crowds adored him, as he strutted the court with an air of wounded pride, bludgeoning in his services and then showing an exquisite touch on his other strokes. Pancho Gonzales was a star, with a star's temperament – volatile, fiery, and vulnerable.

Pancho Gonzales (original spelling, Gonzalez) was born into a poor Mexican family in Los Angeles in 1928. Uncomfortable with authority throughout his life, he skipped school to play tennis, persuading his parents with some difficulty to buy him a racket with which he could compete in tournaments. He was a natural player, with a cannonball service, and a game which combined strong hitting with the most delicate touches. Percentage tennis meant nothing to Gonzales: he played every point to win, often resulting in astonishingly long sets as he refused to succumb. He strutted the court, lambasted officials, and threw his rackets around the locker room. Everybody was just a little afraid of him.

Gonzales won the Southern California championships in 1947, and next year took the national title in three sets from Eric Sturgess of South Africa, the clinching set going to 14-12. In the 1949 US Nationals final he faced the rich and privileged, Ted Schroeder, the very opposite of Gonzales. Gonzales was bitter about the opportunities he never had, and was determined to defeat his upper class opponent. After three sets Schroeder was ahead, mainly because of his unpredictable and varied service, but in the shower break, veteran Frank Shields pointed out to Gonzales that when Schroeder was ahead, he always served a slice instead of a cannonball. Gonzales stalked back, pondering the advice, and when Schroeder went

ABOVE LEFT: *After years in the professional wilderness, Gonzales relished his return to Wimbledon in 1968 aged 40.*

ABOVE RIGHT: *The cannonball serve of Gonzales – at its best virtually unreturnable.*

LEFT: *Looking like a street hustler, Gonzales waits to kill a return from Jaroslav Drobny in 1948 at Forest Hills.*

ABOVE RIGHT: *Gonzales flags during his epic match with Pasarell in 1969.*

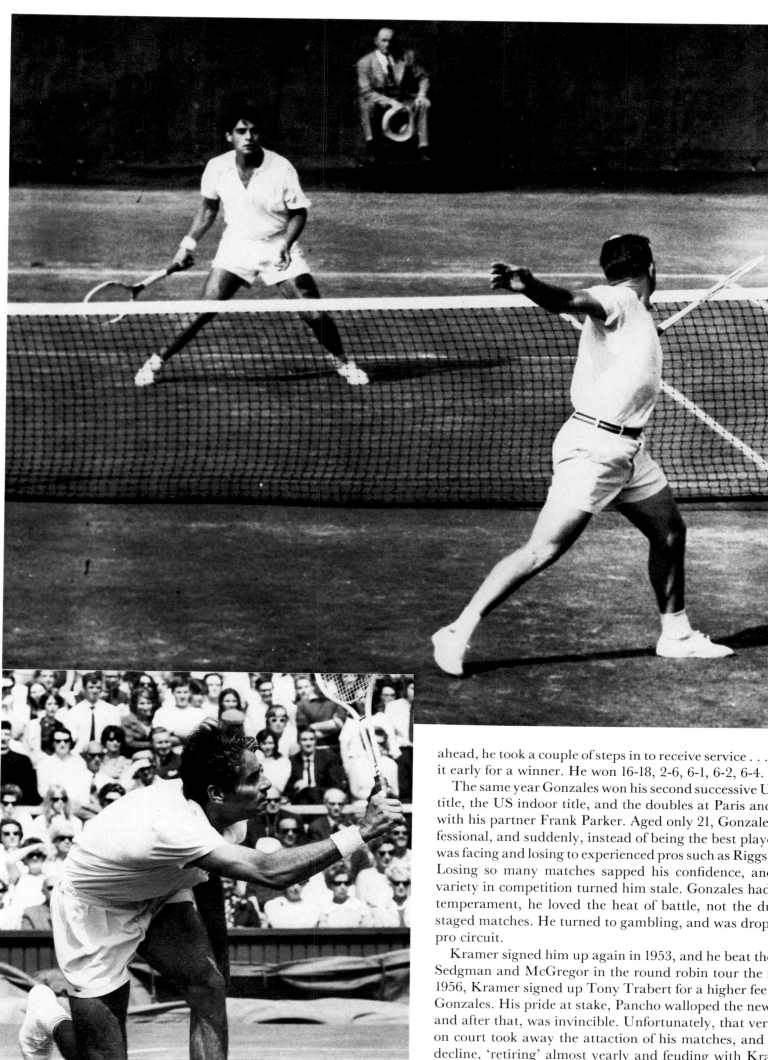

ahead, he took a couple of steps in to receive service . . . and punched it early for a winner. He won 16-18, 2-6, 6-1, 6-2, 6-4.

The same year Gonzales won his second successive US Clay Court title, the US indoor title, and the doubles at Paris and Wimbledon with his partner Frank Parker. Aged only 21, Gonzales turned professional, and suddenly, instead of being the best player around, he was facing and losing to experienced pros such as Riggs and Kramer. Losing so many matches sapped his confidence, and the lack of variety in competition turned him stale. Gonzales had a big match temperament, he loved the heat of battle, not the dull routine of staged matches. He turned to gambling, and was dropped from the pro circuit.

Kramer signed him up again in 1953, and he beat the Australians Sedgman and McGregor in the round robin tour the next year. In 1956, Kramer signed up Tony Trabert for a higher fee than he paid Gonzales. His pride at stake, Pancho walloped the newcomer 74-27 and after that, was invincible. Unfortunately, that very dominance on court took away the attaction of his matches, and he went into decline, 'retiring' almost yearly and feuding with Kramer and his successor Trabert over money.

In 1969, the old lion showed he was still a fighter in his epic first round match against Charlie Pasarell, which went to 112 games. It is tragic that in his prime years – the 1950s and early 1960s – he was lost to mainstream tennis, spending 18 years in night-time arenas. He ranks with Rosewall as one of the best players never to win a Wimbledon singles title.

PART IV
The Global
Circus
1968 onwards

ABOVE: *Graf and Sabatini chat during a break in a doubles game at the French Open.*

Global Expansion

The years since 1968 have, on the whole, been kind to tennis. It has grown to become one of the major participation and spectactor sports in the world with a global appeal – to the extent of being accepted back into the Olympics. But internal politics have blighted the image of the game, and too often media coverage has depicted the sport in terms of greedy players battling with fussy bureaucrats.

Despite the arrival of Open tennis in 1968, the merging of the amateur and professional games was not smooth. World Championship Tennis (WCT) was one early professional tournament which made a major media impact (particularly for its classic 1972 final in which Rosewall magnificently held off Laver), but was resented by the tennis establishment.

The ILTF banned the players WCT had signed from entering its tournaments – thus depriving the likes of John Newcombe the opportunity of competing for the major Grand Slam titles. WCT has since faded in importance, but the political battle between WCT and ILTF in which the players were used as pawns helped to set up the Association of Tennis Professionals (ATP), which in turn led to the Wimbledon boycott of 1973.

The boycott was a saga of poor communication and distrust. It began when Yugoslav player Nikki Pilic was suspended by his national tennis association for missing a Davis Cup match he had allegedly agreed to play. The ATP took up the cudgels on his behalf, while the ILTF backed the Yugoslav body. With no compromise

ABOVE: *Ilie Nastase, one of the great characters of the 1970s, executes a powerful serve.*

BOTTOM: *Switching to a graphite racket gave Evert's game a new, and far more powerful, lease of life.*

FAR RIGHT: *John Newcombe's simple, rugged tennis won him titles and friends around the globe.*

being reached, nearly all the ATP players, with great sadness, boy-cotted the 1973 Wimbledon tournament. The crowds still came, and the championships still ran, but the in-fighting within the tennis world did nothing for the image of the game.

At the head of the ATP as chief executive was Jack Kramer, and it was he who devised what became the foundation of the modern men's game, the Grand Prix circuit, begun in 1970. This was a series of 75 tournaments through the year across the globe, and participat-ing players were set a minimum number of events they must play. A complicated points system picked out the best players, who then contested the Grand Prix Masters Singles (at Madison Square Gar-den) and the Masters Doubles (at London's Royal Albert Hall) to crown the overall champion. The ATP have now taken over running this circuit, which will undergo a number of changes in the future.

Stan Smith won the first Grand Prix Masters, which was decided on a round robin format, and for the following three years, Ilie Nas-tase held the Masters title. McEnroe, Borg and Lendl dominated from 1978, but in 1988 Becker confirmed his status as one of the very top players with a title win over Lendl.

The Virginia Slims World Series circuit uses a broadly similar for-mat for the women's game. After an interrupted start in 1971 (when Billie Jean King won the crown), the first Women's World Series champion in 1977 (and 1978) was Chris Evert, and Tracy Austin has also won it twice; but in the 1980s it was ruled by Martina Nav-ratilova. Steffi Graf took the title in 1987, but lost the 1988 final to Pam Shriver.

With the influence of TV companies on scheduling, the tennis authorities acted in 1970 to avoid overlong matches at tournaments, by introducing a tie break if the score reached 6-6 in all but the final set. After a few variations in the scoring, this has now been standard-ized to make the target seven points, with a minimum two point lead. The innovation has added excitement to hard fought, close matches,

and helps limit the time players spend on court.

While the mechanics of scoring have been amended, the process of hitting a tennis ball has been revolutionized. In 1979 a larger racket head size was introduced, providing a greater 'sweet spot' in the middle of the racket for optimum control, and soon a number of materials (graphite, later mixed with fibreglass, boron, ceramic, kevlar, or metal), started to replace wood as the frame material of the racket. These rackets have brought much greater power to the game, and help make possible a few of the shock results of recent years: few

ABOVE FAR LEFT: *When Stan Smith falls, it's a long way down. However he remained upright long enough to win the Wimbledon title in 1972.*

BELOW LEFT: *Graphite and fibreglass replaced wood in racket manufacture and brought extra power to the game.*

LEFT: *Nikki Pilic, whose suspension by the Yugoslav tennis federation led to players boycotting Wimbledon.*

BELOW: *John Newcombe receives his 1967 Wimbledon trophy, won with the loss of only five games.*

believe that the 17-year-old Becker could have won Wimbledon without his graphite racket, and Evert was unable to seriously challenge Navratilova until she switched from wood to lighter graphite rackets, enabling her to match the force of the Czech's immensely powerful shots.

The players clutching these new, light but explosive rackets in their hands tend to have extra help for their minds too. The professional coach, always a feature of tennis, has risen to new heights of skill and influence: Lendl would be a different player were it not for his coach Tony Roche, and the influence Ion Tiriac had on the Argentine Vilas was legendary – he didn't just provide technical and strategic advice, he ran his life. Top players have no problem paying handsomely for the services of a coach and manager, as prize money has escalated incredibly as tournaments compete to attract the best players.

All the Grand Slam championships have millions of dollars in their prize pots. A top player such as Lendl has won in excess of $13 million (nearly £9 million) so far in his career. As she turned 20, Graf had pulled in more than $4 million (£2.58 million) – in addition to money from endorsements and exhibition matches. So the rewards for reaching the pinnacle of the game are great indeed – but of course so are the pressures.

The most significant new competition to join the many tennis contests was the inclusion of tennis in the Olympic Games at Seoul, 1988, 64 years after the last Olympic tennis match. For two weeks, players battled in the Korean heat not for prize money, but for honor, and the difference in atmosphere from the more mercenary aura of a tournament was refreshing for the players as much as anybody else. Inevitably, Graf won the gold, and Mecir of Czechoslovakia defied his number three seeding to take the men's gold medal.

The fact that neither player is from the great modern fosterers of the game, America or Australia, illustrates the European revolution that took place in the 1980s, when nations such as Sweden, Germany and Czechoslovakia began producing a string of superb players knocking the Americans and Australians off the top of the game. Indeed, in 1988, every Grand Slam title was won by a Swede, and in 1989 Sweden reached its seventh consecutive Davis Cup final.

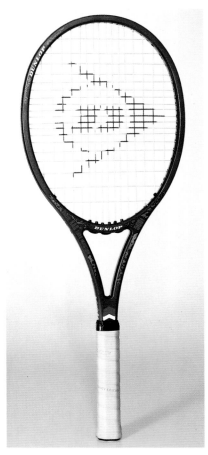

RIGHT: *Dunlop has been at the forefront of the new racket technology.*

BELOW RIGHT: *Steffi Graf celebrates a win at a notable new addition to the tennis circuit – the Olympic Games, 1988.*

BELOW LEFT: *Ivan Lendl at the US Open. His successes here are not matched by his play at Wimbledon.*

FAR RIGHT: *The muscular style of Boris Becker has brought him untold riches, as well as a few injuries.*

The Title Every Player Wants

The first open Wimbledon in 1968 created massive interest among the tennis public as it at last pitched all of the best players in the world against one another. For the professionals, playing at Wimbledon brought credibility and kudos to their careers, for Wimbledon remains a deeply symbolic institution. The public enjoyed seeing some of the most famous names in tennis back at Wimbledon: Gonzales, Rosewall, Hoad, and Laver. In the final Rod Laver easily disposed of Tony Roche and earned the first major prize money given by Wimbledon: £2000, out of the total prize pot of £26,150.

Laver held on to his title with ease the next year, but 1969 is most remembered for the longest-ever Wimbledon match, a first round duel between Pancho Gonzales and Charlie Pasarell. At 41, fiery, tough, Mexican-born Gonzales was a veteran player, but he had never won Wimbledon. Pasarell was 25 and had an appetite for beating top players at Wimbledon – two years before he had defeated reigning champion Manuel Santana in the opening round.

The match began in the early evening, and as the light faded, Gonzales became angry at the referee's refusal to postpone play, losing the first two sets 24-22, 6-1. The next day, he re-started the fight, winning the third set 16-14, and the fourth 6-3. Pasarell then took a grip and had seven match points, but he could not finish off the veteran player, and eventually Gonzales took the set 11-9. At five hours 12 minutes, and 112 games, it remains the longest men's singles game at Wimbledon – a record that should stand forever as tie breaks were introduced in 1971, partly as a result of this marathon.

Laver lost his title in 1970 with a surprise defeat by Britain's Roger Taylor, much to the delight of the crowd, and the men's final the same year was an exciting duel between Australians John Newcombe and the crowd's favorite, strokemaker Ken Rosewall. Newcombe won and retained the crown the next year.

In 1972, international tennis politics led to a break between the International Lawn Tennis Federation (ILTF) and the World Championship Tennis (WCT) organization run by the Texan Lamar Hunt. No contract pros competed at Wimbledon that year, although the tournament resulted in a thrilling final, delayed by rain to the Sunday, between the lanky American Stan Smith and the irrepressible, unpredictable Romanian Ilie Nastase. Nervous Nastase,

in his first Wimbledon singles final, kept switching rackets and plucking anxiously at the racket strings between points, but his superb touch play put him one set up. Californian Smith was the exact opposite: tall, possessing a powerful serve and relying on his consistency to wear down his opponent. At two sets all, four games all, Smith lost the first two points on his service but a fluke volley stopped the rot and he swept through the next three games to become champion.

Politics intruded again in 1973, when the newly formed Association of Tennis Professionals (ATP) viewed the suspension of Nikki Pilic by his tennis association as a point of principle, and flexed its muscles with a boycott of Wimbledon. The men's tournament was decimated but crowds still flocked to see some excellent play, culminating in the only all Eastern bloc final to date between Czech Jan Kodes and Alex Metreveli of the Soviet Union. In the doubles, a formidable pairing of Nastase and Jimmy Connors took the title with flamboyant play.

Connors was back to take the singles title the next year in a one-sided final against one of the greatest players never to win Wimbledon, Ken Rosewall. As the Australian veteran gracefully stroked his way through the early rounds, many sentimentalists hoped he would at last get the title. But at 40, playing an abrasive, hard hitting 21-year-old, he did not make a real contest of it.

Connors looked set for a long run of Wimbledon championships as he took on Arthur Ashe in the 1975 final, but the underdog turned the tables with one of the bravest tactical displays in tennis history. Like Connors, Ashe usually played fast and furious, but he realized that if he fed the young champion pace, he would be swamped. So the 32-year-old changed his style of play entirely, floating angled balls for Connors to bludgeon back. During breaks of play he sat motionless, looking as if he was in a trance, while his bemused opponent fidgeted in his seat. Ashe's win was the first by a black man in a Wimbledon men's final, and one of the best displays of tactical tennis.

1976 saw the beginning of the Borg era; his heavy topspin drives taking him to the first of five successive men's titles. He also equalled the achievements of Don Budge (1938), Tony Trabert (1955) and Chuck McKinley (1963), by winning the title without losing a set. The key matches in his remarkable five year reign are described later in the book.

John McEnroe finally beat Borg for the 1981 championship, but such was his controversial behavior that the All England committee broke with tradition by declining to offer him the life membership all champions have enjoyed in the past.

In 1982 Jimmy Connors beat McEnroe for the singles title he had originally won eight years previously, both players demonstrating their propensity for on court outbursts in a grueling four hour 16 minute contest. McEnroe was back in the final the next year to defeat a surprise opponent, Chris Lewis of New Zealand, and this time the committee saw fit to offer McEnroe life membership. He responded the following year with a 6-1, 6-1, 6-2 trouncing of Connors.

In 1985 Boris Becker sent every pundit scurrying for the record

books. His remarkable men's title win was the first by an unseeded player, the first by a German, and at 17 he was the youngest-ever winner. His ferocious serves and ruthless drives and volleys were too much for Kevin Curren, and for Ivan Lendl the next year too.

1987 produced one of the more memorable moments at a Wimbledon final. Pat Cash proved too tough at grass court play for Ivan Lendl, and celebrated his win by climbing up in the stands to embrace his father. It was an emotional sight that had Centre Court cheering the gutsy Australian.

Becker was back in the final in 1988, but Swede Stefan Edberg, who some had said did not have the personality of a major winner, handled the German's vicious serve brilliantly to take the title. The same two players contested the 1989 final, but Becker had found even more pace in his shots and a subdued Edberg lost in a disappointingly one sided match.

Turning to the women's game, in 1968 Billie Jean King retained her title for the third year running, and the next year faced Britain's Ann Jones to keep it. Thirty years old, Ann Jones (née Haydon) was an ex-table tennis champion with a dogged style lit by flashes of bril-

LEFT: *Rod Laver's left-handed aggressive style of play confounded his opponents and took him to the top of his profession.*

BELOW: *Boris Becker tosses his racket between points. Usually a fairly calm player, he is occasionally prone to outburst of emotion.*

BELOW LEFT: *Ken Rosewall at his last Wimbledon in 1974. He never won the all-England title.*

BELOW RIGHT: *Margaret Court's athleticism boosted a tennis talent that needed constant practice to stay at the top.*

liance. The professional circuit had toughened up her play and she surprised Billie Jean King by recovering from losing the first 22 game set and, noisily backed by the crowd, took the match.

Billie Jean was back in 1970 to fight one of the most famous Wimbledon finals, against Margaret Court. Over two hours 27 minutes, and 46 games (breaking the 1919 record for longest final), the standard of play rarely dropped below the superb. King led on serve through the first set but lost it 14-12; Court had a match point at 7-6 and four more at 10-9 before she won. Margaret Court reached all three finals in 1971, but lost each one. Her singles crown was taken by a player Wimbledon had taken to its heart, the elegant, graceful, infuriatingly erratic Evonne Goolagong. She crushed Margaret Court in 1971, losing only five games in a superlative display.

In the 1972 semi-final Goolagong met a 17-year-old American making her Wimbledon debut amid great publicity. Chris Evert was already being touted as a future Wimbledon champion, but the Aus-

LEFT: *Bjorn Borg admires the championship trophy for the first time in 1976. He kept it for five years.*

BELOW: *Pat Cash, who won the title in 1987, immediately endeared himself to the crowd by climbing the stands to embrace his father.*

tralian recovered from being a set and 0-3 down by playing short to the weak Evert backhand. In the final, a revitalized Billie Jean King swept Miss Goolagong aside 6-3, 6-3.

The men's boycott in 1973 focused more attention on the women's tournament, which produced its first all-American final for 16 years. Chris Evert was perhaps overawed by the Centre Court occasion and the unstoppable Mrs King collected her fifth singles title, and the triple crown. She won her sixth singles in 1976, a win sandwiched between two championships for Chris Evert, the second a close fought meeting with Mrs Evonne Cawley (née Goolagong).

1977 was a great occasion for Wimbledon as it celebrated its centenary and the Queen's Silver Jubilee. Many past champions attended, and there were nostalgic appearances by Bueno, Susman and Jones. All Britain prayed for a win in this historic year, and there was delight as both Virginia Wade and Sue Barker reached the semi-finals. Only Virginia Wade reached the final, and everyone wondered whether it would be Virginia's year. The question was understandable, for this was her 16th Wimbledon and she had never reached the singles final, failing to reproduce the brilliant rhythmic tennis with which she won many other tournaments, including the US, Australian and Italian championships. As she nervously lost the first set to the Netherland's Betty Stove, the crowd feared the worst. But she pulled herself and her game together and won the next two sets, prompting the rejoicing Centre Court to yell several choruses of 'For she's a jolly good fellow'.

Martina Navratilova won her first title the next year, beating Chris Evert, and repeated her win in 1979. 1980 saw a finals upset when Evonne Cawley, now nearly 30, re-captured the title after eight

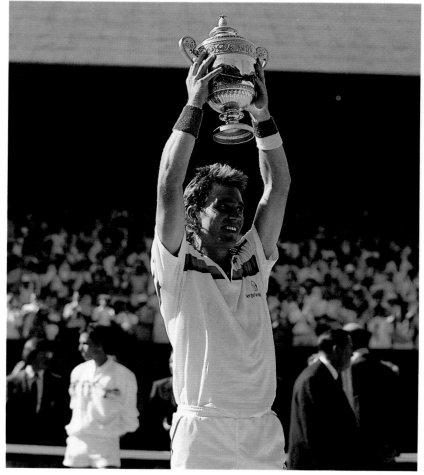

years with a two set win over Chris Evert clinched on a tiebreaker.

After Chris Evert won again in 1981, Martina Navratilova began a sequence of six consecutive title wins during which she often completely outclassed her opponents. The run ended in a thrilling win in 1988 by the young German Steffi Graf, who repeated the victory much more easily the following year.

Although now the only major trophy contested on grass, Wimbledon remains the title every player wants to win. Ivan Lendl who has never won this singles title, intends to skip the 1990 French Open to get more practice on grass for his title challenge, for example. With a village of hospitality tents sprouting up every year, and ever increasing crowds, the tournament is also a major fund raiser for British tennis.

ABOVE LEFT: *McEnroe in a familiar scenario, arguing with the umpire during his 1980 semi-final against Connors.*

FAR LEFT: *Chris Evert shows her irritation at a decision, while her opponent Virginia Wade keeps up her concentration for her semi-final win in 1977.*

LEFT: *Spot the winner. King crosses the net to congratulate Ann Jones, who beat her in the 1969 final.*

ABOVE: *Typical athleticism from the muscular Navratilova, who has won eight Wimbledon titles.*

ABOVE RIGHT: *Evonne Goolagong captured many hearts, as well as a few titles with her graceful and carefree style.*

RIGHT: *Unusual gymnastics from Lendl in yet another attempt to win the Wimbledon crown.*

Keep Off The Grass

The first US championship to accept entries from professional players had an appropriate absurdity at its finish. After Arthur Ashe had defeated Tom Okker 14-12, 5-7, 6-3, 3-6, 6-3, the $14,000 prize money was handed to . . . Okker, because Ashe was still an amateur. Since then the US Open has switched surfaces twice, grown in status and importance, and become heavily influenced by the demands of television and sponsors, particularly in the scheduling of matches. Meanwhile, tennis in America has seem many changes since 1968: the growth in acceptance of the women's game, the birth of team tennis, and the setting up of the Grand Prix.

For the first two years, the US Open at Forest Hills was staged two weeks after the amateur-only National Championships, which were finally dropped in 1970 (Ashe won both titles in 1968). Australia's Tony Roche was the losing finalist in 1969 and 1970, first to Rod Laver, completing his Grand Slam, and then to Ken Rosewall. Rosewall made the final again in 1974, but was crushed by Jimmy Connors with the loss of only two games. After that championship, the grass of Forest Hills – which had been a notoriously unreliable surface – was dug up, to be replaced by a patented 'clay court', made up of granite chippings. The new surface was slower and favored the strong groundstrokes of clay specialists, such as Manuel Orantes (who recovered from being two sets to one and 0-5 down against Guillermo Vilas to reach the final and easily beat Connors) and Vilas, who beat Connors in 1977.

However, it was becoming clear that the US Open was outgrowing its West Hills home, and for the 1978 tournament a massive new venue was built at Flushing Meadow. This has a stadium capacity of 20,000, but is plagued by the noise of planes landing or taking off from the nearby La Guardia Airport. The best news for the American players was that the acrylic cement court at Flushing Meadow had more pace and bounce than clay, and was more suited to their style of play. Jimmy Connors' three set victory over Borg that year showed his capacity to adapt to all surfaces: in his five successive finals, he had won the US title once each on grass, clay, and now cement.

Over the next three years John McEnroe became the first player to win the US singles title three times in a row since Bill Tilden, beating Gerulaitis once and Borg twice; his 1980 encounter with the Swede was an epic five setter, which McEnroe won 7-6, 6-1, 6-7, 5-7, 6-4. Connors was back in front for the next couple of years, and in 1984 McEnroe won again, with this trio of finals having the loser in common: Ivan Lendl.

Lendl was born in 1960 in Czechoslovakia, but now lives in the US and has applied for American citizenship. A tremendously hard hitter of the ball, Lendl is a highly skilled, fit, and determined opponent. Efficient rather than spectacular, he plays mainly from the baseline, and has a powerful service. In the tennis directories, Lendl is followed alphabetically by Suzanne Lenglen, and the contrast could not be greater: Lenglen was glamorous, startling, and brought a buzz everywhere she performed, while Lendl, for all his years at the pinnacle of the game, has not endeared himself to the crowds with his dour image. A top ten player since 1980, Lendl finally took the US

ABOVE FAR LEFT: *Typical fire from the inspirational Guillermo Vilas.*

ABOVE LEFT: *A beleaguered Tony Roche, who never won a US title, losing both the 1969 and 1970 finals.*

BELOW LEFT: *Surprise 1975 winner Manuel Orantes of Spain lifts the US trophy after his three set win over Connors.*

LEFT: *Tom Okker returns to Arthur Ashe at the start of the first US Open final in 1968.*

BELOW: *The only way to clear excess water from the rubberized surface of Flushing Meadow is with a broom.*

title in his fourth consecutive final in 1985, when he beat John McEnroe in straight sets. The gaunt faced Czech took the title for the next two years, losing only six games to Mecir in 1986, and defeating Wilander in 1987. The Swede took his revenge the following year when he won a tough five setter against Lendl. In 1989 Lendl reached his eighth consecutive US Open final, but could not control the fierce power of Becker, and lost in four sets. With his 1989 Australian title win, Lendl has clinched every Grand Slam championship except Wimbledon, where he simply cannot adjust to the fast grass – although he learned to play superbly on the cement of Flushing Meadow, which performs like a cross between clay and grass.

FAR LEFT: *John McEnroe shows his jubilation at his fourth US singles title win in 1984 over Ivan Lendl.*

BOTTOM LEFT: *Ivan Lendl looks strained during his 6-7, 6-0, 7-6, 6-4 Flushing Meadow win over Mats Wilander in 1987 . . .*

LEFT: *. . . Wilander's revenge the next year, after a five-set final.*

RIGHT: *Evonne Goolagong had more success at Wimbledon, and never won the US Open – but it took players of the caliber of Court, King and Evert to deny her in four successive finals.*

Virginia Wade of Britain was the first winner of the US Open women's title. Using her superb service to beat Billie Jean King in two sets, she gained the first British win in the American championships since Betty Nuthall in 1930. For the next six years Mrs King and Margaret Court each clinched the title three times.

In 1975 Chris Evert began a long run of successes in the competition, by overcoming Evonne Goolagong in a tight, three set final – a case of *déjà vu* for Goolagong, for she had lost the previous two finals, all closely fought to the last set.

Chris Evert's reign was interrupted by a girl who had modeled her game on Evert herself, Tracy Austin. Possessing an even temperament, great tenacity, and consistent groundstrokes, Tracy Austin mirrored her idol Evert, and in 1979 defeated her in two sets. Two years later Austin was back to beat Martina Navratilova in a match decided by tie breaks in the last two sets, and would certainly have collected many more major titles if she had not stopped playing at the age of 20. Back trouble caused the break, but the precocious youngster also seemed to be burned out, having been playing top level tennis for six years already. A comeback attempt in 1989 was stymied by a car accident.

By 1983 Chris Evert had taken her toll of singles titles to six, but lost that year's final to her long time friend and rival Martina Navratilova. The Czech-born Navratilova had acquired American citizenship two years before, and was desperate to win her new national championship. Having lost in a tie break to Austin two years before, she made the most of her opportunity this time, and the win was the first of four US Open titles for her in six finals. She lost in 1985 to Hana Mandlikova, however, recovering the next year to beat Helena Sukova (also Czech-born) in 1986, a year when all the singles finalists came from Czechoslovakia (Lendl beat Mecir for the men's title).

In 1988, Steffi Graf took her first US title with a three sets win over

her doubles partner Gabriela Sabatini. She defeated her again in the 1989 semi-final, before outgunning Navratilova to retain the title. A new era in US women's champions had begun.

That women's tennis is treated more or less on a par with the men's game is due to the efforts of a band of players early in the 1970s. In 1970, Gladys Heldman, publisher of *World Tennis*, was sufficiently appalled by the much lower prize money offered in the women's game that she organized, in a matter of a few weeks, an eight strong women's tournament in Houston. She signed up eight top players for a dollar each, and proved with the success of the event that women's tennis could be as much of a draw as the men's game. The result was the development of the Virginia Slim women's circuit, now a mainstay of the game worldwide, which culminates in the Virginia Slim Championships. In those early years, Billie Jean King was a dynamic publicisizer of the women's circuit, and the arrival of pretty, elegant and poised Chris Evert helped to win over the public to the cause.

Team tennis, already established as the format for the Davis Cup and other international contests, had a brief stint of popularity in the USA from 1974. World Team Tennis pitched teams representing American cities against each other in a series of league matches where spectators were encouraged to yell and shout for their favorites. WTT helped to build tennis as an entertainment sport, but fizzled out in competition with existing attractions.

ABOVE LEFT: *A rueful Evert congratulates Tracy Austin in 1979, who aped the champion's style and beat her in two 90-minute sets.*

BOTTOM LEFT: *A familiar sight through the 1980s: Evert and Navratilova at the close of yet another contest.*

LEFT: *Powerful German Steffi Graf lost to Navratilova in 1987, but took the US title for the next two years, and looks set for a few more.*

BELOW: *Evert picked up six US singles titles in her career.*

Australia Bounces Back

The story of the Australian Open after 1968 is one of early decline, followed by a rise in fortunes as it gained acceptance as an important tournament. It now attracts an international field eager to launch their Grand Slam attempts from the huge new Flinders Park stadium in Melbourne. Until 1976, an Australian reached every final, winning eight of them, but since then the title has gone abroad each year, despite some valiant efforts from Pat Cash.

The first Australian Open took place in Brisbane, and was won by Rod Laver on his way to his second Grand Slam. After 1972 the tournament was held in Melbourne, changing sites in 1988 from Kooyong to Flinders Park, and the traditional grass has been dropped in favor of a hard, rubberized surface.

The 1972 tournament was the last time Ken Rosewall won the singles title, beating fellow veteran Malcolm Anderson in three sets. The next year's champion, John Newcombe, kept his career going as long as Rosewall's, and in the early 1970s, after 10 years in top tennis, he was still a formidable performer.

Newcombe played a rugged, simple, serve-volley game with a no-nonsense approach so successfully that he was named 'Player of the Year' in 1967, four years after his debut as a 19-year-old in the Davis Cup. He won the Wimbledon singles three times (in 1967, 1970 and 1971), two US championships (1967 and 1973), and the Australian title in 1973 and 1975. Surprisingly, given his fast playing style, he also had victories on clay in the German Open 1968 and Italian Open 1969. Partnered with Tony Roche, he won five Wimbledon

doubles titles (including the first hattrick of titles since the Dohertys in 1903-5), four Australian, two French and one US. The pair are remembered for their superb doubles play and the sense of humor they injected into it, as well as the partying frolics they found energy for.

1977 was a strange year for the Australian Open because everything happened twice. Anxious to maintain the tournament as a Grand Slam event, the organizers moved it from January to December to avoid a clash with the Grand Prix Masters in America. In 1986 it returned to January, to accommodate a date shift by the Masters. The early 1980s saw another crisis as the tournament failed to attract enough high-caliber players. This is illustrated by the two successive title wins of South Africa's Johan Kriek, both finals being against the American Steve Denton – battles between two of tennis's journeymen.

Australian women's tennis had faced a similar problem in the late 1970s, where the only shining light in the desert left by the decline of Margaret Court was the elegant Evonne Goolagong. Born in the New South Wales outback, Evonne Goolagong learned tennis with a rope stretched between two trees as a net, and was spotted by Australian coach Vic Edwards, who became her legal guardian. Her tennis was graceful and although she did not hit the ball hard, her volleys were superb and she was capable of outrageous angled shots which bemused her opponents as much as they delighted the crowd. Her legendary lapses of concentration were dubbed 'walkabouts' in reference to her partly aboriginal ancestory.

Having lost three consecutive finals (twice to Margaret Court and once to Britain's Virginia Wade) Goolagong swept the Australian women's singles title four times between 1974 and 1978, missing the 1977 season to have a baby. Her carefree attitude probably stopped her achieving more successes, but it was a refreshing reminder of earlier days of tennis, and she enchanted spectators wherever she played.

The solution to the problems of the women's championship in the 1970s was to separate it from the men's tournament, forcing it to stand and fight for its survival at international level. The upgraded tournament succeeded in attracting players of the quality of Mandlikova, Navratilova, and Evert (the three champions from 1980 onwards), and in 1983 the refreshed tournament was merged with the men's competition as a major Grand Slam event.

That year the Australian Open truly came of age, equal in prestige

ABOVE LEFT: *Mats Wilander's baseline style won him three titles down under, the last a five-set win over Pat Cash in 1988.*

ABOVE: *Margaret Court turned herself into the greatest Australian woman player with incessant practice, and won 11 of her country's singles titles.*

LEFT: *Court's successor, Evonne Goolagong had the killer instinct, too, as is shown by this shot of Virginia Wade, prostrate during her 1975 semi-final duel with Goolagong.*

RIGHT: *Czech-born Hana Mandlikova has rarely fulfilled her true potential, except in 1980 and 1986, when she won the Australian Open.*

and prize money to the other three major championships. The men's champion was the young Swede Mats Wilander, beating Ivan Lendl in straight sets. Within two years it was clear that the Kooyong, even with its 20,000 seater stadium court, could not accommodate the championships for much longer, and a six hectare site at Flinders Park, still in Melbourne, was acquired. The Open made its debut at Flinders Park in 1988, using a cushioned surface composed of polyurethane and rubber, housed in a stadium which has the option of a retractable roof if the weather is bad. The surface is roughly equivalent to grass, but with a higher bounce. The stadium heats to very high temperatures in the Australian sun, and players douse themselves with iced water during breaks in play to offset dehydration. Wilander won his third title in the first men's final at the new venue, frustrating Pat Cash who, for the second year running lost a five set final in his own championship (Edberg beat him in 1987). The following year Ivan Lendl finally won the Australian title, at his seventh attempt, in a straight sets win over his fellow Czechoslovak Miloslav Mecir.

Steffi Graf took the Australian women's title in 1988 and 1989, keeping Chris Evert out 6-1, 7-6 in her Grand Slam year, and then beating Helena Sukova in 71 minutes – the first of her contests to take more than an hour to play.

Flinders Park is the centre for Tennis Australia (the official Australian tennis body) in its development of new talent. No Australian has won a singles title in their own championships since Evonne Cawley (née Goolagong) in 1977, and many hopes are focused on that magnificent new stadium.

BELOW LEFT: *Pat Cash became a national hero after his 1987 Wimbledon win – but he lost both his Australian Open finals.*

BELOW: *Stefan Edberg gets treatment for cramp during his 1989 title attempt.*

BOTTOM: *Flinders Park, venue for the Australian Open since 1988, features a retractable roof.*

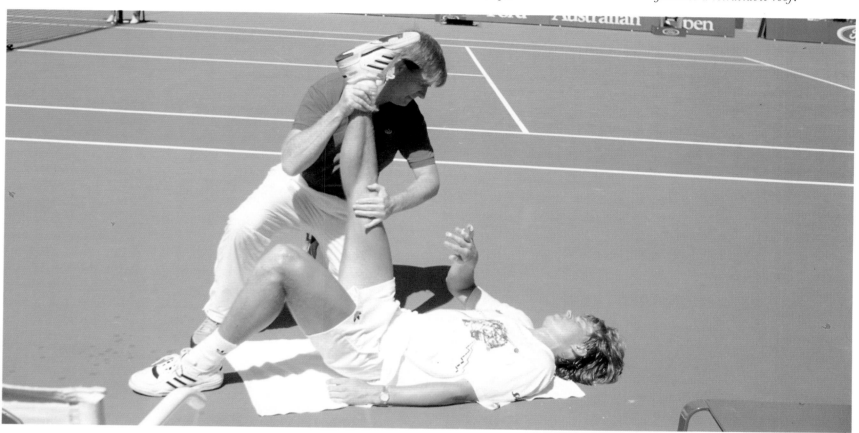

The Toughest Challenge

Some players believe the French Open is the hardest tournament to win – and the most enjoyable to attend. The slow red clay of the Stade Roland Garros takes the pace off the ball, putting the accent on rallying skills, on angled shots, and outwitting the opponent. However, when two baseliners slug out a long match on clay, the game can become less like physical chess and more like watching a pendulum swing. For spectators and players, the surroundings and facilities are excellent, and everyone loves to be in Paris in the springtime. The surprise singles titles winners in the vintage year of 1989, Sanchez and Chang, are evidence of a new strength in the clay court game which augers well for some great contests in the future.

The 1968 French Open was the first Grand Slam event in which professionals could take part. Ken Rosewall took advantage of this to take his second French title, 15 years after his first, against Rod Laver. The same two players reached the opposite result the following year, but Laver had struggled to reach the final and the championship was the toughest of the four Grand Slam titles he took that year.

The next two finals were East European affairs, Czech Jan Kodes beating Yugoslavian Zeljko Franulovic one year and Romanian Ilie Nastase the next, but in 1974 Bjorn Borg took the first of six French titles just after his 18th birthday. His patient style of play was perfectly suited to slow clay, but he had to make a remarkable recovery against Manuel Orantes in that first final. Two sets down, he suddenly hit the right groove and took the match with the loss of only two further games.

Over the following years Borg won finals against superb clay court players such as Vilas and Lendl. Another Swede, Mats Wilander, exploded on to the tennis scene in 1982, the year Borg did not defend his title. Wilander had won the junior title 12 months previously, but this time he beat Lendl 4-6, 7-5, 3-6, 6-4, 6-2, Gerulaitis 6-3, 6-3, 4-6, 6-4, Jose Luis Clerc 7-5, 6-2, 1-6, 7-5 and, in the final, Guillermo Vilas 1-6, 7-6 (saving one set point) 6-0, 6-4 to take the men's title. He was the first unseeded player to win a Grand Slam title in the Open tennis era.

A right-hander, with a double-handed backhand, Wilander is a

ABOVE: *Arantxa Sanchez's 1989 French Open triumph was a boost for tennis, and launched her ebullient personality into the top ranks of the game.*

RIGHT: *Bjorn Borg never lost a French Open final. His style of play was perfectly suited to slow clay, and earned him six titles.*

FAR RIGHT: *Guillermo Vilas demolished Brian Gottfried 6-0, 6-3, 6-0 in 1977, but lost his other three finals, two to Borg and one to Wilander.*

ABOVE: *To the undiluted joy of the French crowd, Yannick Noah (right) defeated Sweden's Mats Wilander (left) 6-2, 7-5, 7-6 in 1983 to become the first Frenchman to win his national title for 37 years.*

RIGHT: *Three times French Open winner Ivan Lendl, who beat McEnroe over five sets for his first title in 1984.*

RIGHT: *Yannick Noah's talent was spotted by Arthur Ashe, and he became French junior champion in 1977. Always a great crowd pleaser, he has won his national singles and (with Leconte) doubles title once, and reached the quarter-finals four times.*

determined, adept baseliner who rises to big occasions but can be moody and erratic. He repeated his title win in 1985 by defeating Lendl, and again in 1988 with a win over Henri Leconte. That year he was named official world champion after winning every Grand Slam event except Wimbledon, having improved his service and volleying.

None of Wilander's wins received the applause given to the 1983 victor Yannick Noah, who had become the first Frenchman to win his national title for 37 years. He beat the title holder, Mats Wilander in straight sets, taking the third on a tie break. Born in France but brought up in the Cameroons, Noah was spotted by Arthur Ashe during a tour of Africa, and given the support he needed to reach top tennis. France had reached the Davis Cup final the previous year, and with players like Noah, Henri Leconte, Thierry Tulasne and Guy Forget has begun to produce its best crop of players since the Four Musketeers in the 1920s. That said, none have been able to re-

LEFT: *Coached by Brian Gottfried, Michael Chang was the youngest player to compete in the US Open since 1918, at 15 years 6 months. His wins over Lendl and then Edberg in 1989 sent shock waves through the tennis world, and he became the first American to take the French title for 34 years.*

RIGHT: *The players love the French Open, with its good facilities and knowledgeable crowd. Here Connors and Gerulaitis (losing finalist in 1980) are obviously enjoying their stay.*

LEFT: *Evert and Navratilova fought some memorable French Open finals, meeting four times. Evert usually had the upper hand on the slow surface.*

RIGHT: *Part of the razzmatazz of modern tennis is the speeches by players straight after the final. After their three hour marathon, Graf and Sanchez were remarkably composed, and Graf was generous in her praise for the sparky Spaniard.*

peat that French title win, although Leconte reached the final in 1988.

The 1984 decider saw John McEnroe win the first two sets against Ivan Lendl, but he lost momentum and the Czech fought back to take his first French title 3-6, 2-6, 6-4, 6-2, 6-2. Lendl lost the final in 1985 too, but won in 1986 and 1987.

In 1989 Lendl was sensationally ousted in the fourth round by 17-year-old American Michael Chang. Agile, quick about the court and a great returner of serve, Chang (son of Taiwanese parents) very nearly lost to Lendl, but showed great resilience to come back from two sets down. Reaching the final, he returned Stefan Edberg's powerful service incredibly well to take the championship 6-1, 3-6, 3-6, 6-4, 6-2: he was the first American to take the French men's title since Tony Trabert in 1955.

Chris Evert stands out in the French Open women's singles role of honor. Her shrewd baseline game was ideally suited to the slow red clay of Stade Roland Garros, and she took the title seven times from 1974 to 1986 – and that period included three years when she did not play, being committed to Team Tennis in America. She very nearly began her run of wins a year earlier, losing a tight final 6-7, 7-6, 6-4 to

Court in 1973.

Britain, Yugoslavia and Romania grabbed the trophy from 1976 to 1978, with Sue Barker, Mima Jausovec and Virginia Ruzici taking the title. Other winners in recent years have been Hana Mandlikova in 1981 and Martina Navratilova in 1984 (her Grand Slam year), but Navratilova lost the following three finals, twice to Evert and in 1987 to Graf 6-4, 4-6, 8-6.

The best equipped of modern women players, Graf's powerful game proved embarrassingly strong in the 1988 championship when she slaughtered Natalia Zvereva without losing a game, in 32 minutes. It was hardly a great spectacle for the crowd, and few predicted the result would be much different in 1989 when the formidable West German faced 17-year-old Arantxa Sanchez. The cheery Spanish girl had drawn comfort from Chang's unexpected win against Edberg, and from the sight of 15-year-old Monica Seles taking a set off Graf in the semi-finals. She saved set points to take the opening set tie break, lost the second, and was 5-3 down in the third. But Sanchez has great self-belief, and she lost only three points in a brilliant surge to win 7-6, 3-6, 7-5. It had taken almost three nerve-wracking hours, and the crowd went wild.

The Davis Cup under threat

With the coming of open tennis, the Davis Cup suffered by continuing to bar professional players for five years, depriving itself of some of the top players at a time when the public could enjoy watching them perform in other competitions against all comers. The crowds were smaller and the contest was becoming devalued. Politics was also an underlying theme as many countries refused to play against South Africa because they objected to its apartheid system. South Africa won on default in 1974 when India refused to play her, in a year when Sweden's tie with Chile was played virtually in private to avoid disruption by demonstrators angry at the military junta's takeover. In the next three years, 15 nations withdrew from the contest for political reasons. Clearly the Davis Cup, for all its founder's ideals, was suffering, and the committee of management ruled that any defaulter would be barred for the following year. South Africa was banned from the Cup in 1980.

The Challenge Round format was ended in 1972. Now the cup holder had to fight through to the final, a move which ended a massive advantage for the holder which had been built into the Davis Cup since it began. The result was a much more open contest and over the next decade relative newcomers Sweden, Italy and Czechoslovakia, all captured the cup for the first time. Equally significant was the rising entry count during this period: nearly 60 nations during the 1970s. Fifty years before, the entry figure was six.

The Australians had reached every challenge round since 1937, but in 1969 they lost ignominiously to Mexico in the opening tie of the American Zone, ending a long period of domination. That year America successfully defended the cup for the first time in 22 years by beating Romania 5-0, when Ashe and Stan Smith defeated the talented youngster Nastase and the veteran Tiriac in the singles. The next year they achieved a similar rout over the West Germans, and in 1971 were faced with an intimidating atmosphere in Romania for the challenge round. Reigning US Open champion Smith began by

beating Nastase in staight sets, with only the first of them a real contest (Nastase fought back from 0-5). Smith also outclassed Tiriac in three sets, and the US kept the Cup.

In 1972 – the first without the challenge round – America again faced the Romanians for the final. With America 2-1 up, Smith faced Tiriac in a crucial and controversial match. Tiriac varied his shots to unsettle Smith, who loved to volley from the net. Smith also had to cope with some poor calling by the Romanian officials and commented that he had learnt to hit everything back, however far out it was, just in case. The match swung both ways before a calm Smith won the final set to love. Given the circumstances the match was played in, it was a remarkable achievement.

LEFT: *Sweden's victorious Davis Cup team of 1975.*

ABOVE: *Sporting their Davis Cup blazers are Stan Smith and Bob Lutz, who were blitzed by Mexico in 1975.*

ABOVE RIGHT: *Raul Ramirez (right) performed heroically in his country's amazing 1975 defeat of America.*

BELOW RIGHT: *Ivan Lendl helped the Czechs to a 4-1 win over Italy in 1980. If he becomes a US citizen, he could play against his old country – as Navratilova has done in the Federation Cup.*

In 1973 professionals were at last allowed into the Davis Cup, a move that probably saved the competition from a slow death. The Australians were able to field a team including veterans John Newcombe, Ken Rosewall and Rod Laver. In one of the best finals ever, they met the Americans in Cleveland and, surprisingly, Rosewall never got on the court – Newcombe and Laver played marvelous tennis, and formed an unstoppable doubles pairing. The matches were close, though. First Newcombe just beat Smith, who lost in the worst possible way: a double fault on his own service as he gambled on hitting down the middle. Then Tom Gorman played brilliantly to challenge Rod Laver, going two sets to one up, but the experienced Australian stuck with his shots and turned the match. The eventual 5-0 score reflected the strength and confidence of the Australians, but seems hard on an American team that went down fighting.

America was humiliated in 1975 partly because top players had not made themselves available to play, and partly because of the brilliance of Raul Ramirez against Smith, and superb teamwork by Ramirez and Zarazua against Stockton and Lutz. That year, in the first all-European final since 1933, Sweden met Czechoslovakia in

Stockholm. Borg steamrollered first Hebrec and then Kodes in straight sets, and in between these matches, teamed up with Bengston to beat Kodes who had been mis-paired with Zednik, in the doubles. The whole of Sweden rejoiced. It was only the sixth nation ever to have won the Davis Cup. A seventh name was added the following year. An Italian team led by Panatta proved too strong for the Chileans even on their home territory in Santiago. Team captain Pietrangeli did a lap of honour holding the famous cup, pursued by his players waving little Italian flags.

In 1977 Australia was pitted against Argentina in the inter-zone final. A fascinating ploy was tried in the doubles that rivals the American 'scissors system' of the 1950s: when Vilas or Cano were serving, the non-server would stand two yards from the net, right on the center line. Immediately the ball was struck, he would nip sideways and the server would race up to fill in the gap. Alexander and Dent found themselves watching their opponent's movements more than the ball. At two-all in the final set, the match was postponed until the next day. The overnight break allowed them to collect their thoughts and the Australians won the last four games.

In the final Italy took Australia all the way with the tie hinging on the final singles between two strong and fit players: the solid, even tempered Alexander, and the dashing, unpredictable Panatta. The match see-sawed until it reached the fifth set, five games all. Then Alexander's determined scuttling for every shot took its toll on the flamboyant Pannatta, and Australia won 9-7.

By this stage, the Davis Cup was having difficulty attracting the top players from every country to compete, as participating involved making a financial sacrifice, and missing lucrative exhibitions or tournaments. Players of the caliber of Connors and Borg were simply not making themselves available, and crowds began to fall off. With America failing to even come close to winning the cup, no major sponsor was likely to back the contest. After 80 years, the Davis Cup was under threat. An unlikely savior emerged in the person of John McEnroe. He consistently agreed to play Davis Cup ties for the USA, and some commentators believe his loyalty to the competition which helped to maintain its high standard of tennis and attraction for spectators, rescued it from serious decline.

America won the Davis Cup four times in the next six years facing, in 1978, a surprise team in the final: Great Britain, who had defeated a shocked Australia at the previous hurdle. McEnroe easily beat John Lloyd in the first tie, but then Brian Gottfried was overtaken by the gutsy Buster Mottram, who saved a match point in the course of winning in five sets. The Americans killed off the challengers after

that, with McEnroe setting a new record for conceding the least number of games (only 10) in the final round. The next year the American team ruthlessly disposed of Italy without dropping a set.

In 1980 Italy reached the final round again, to be met by Czechoslovakia in Prague. The noisy Italian fans were outraged by some of the umpiring decisions as the Czechs swept to victory, and became the first East European country to hold the Cup.

The following year the future of the Davis Cup was finally secured

ABOVE: *John Lloyd's best efforts were not enough to overcome the Americans in the 1978 final.*

LEFT: *Stan Smith, team trainer Tony Trabert, and John McEnroe celebrate their 4-1 win over Britain, who had beaten France, Czechoslovakia, and Australia to reach the final.*

ABOVE: *Yannick Noah takes a tumble. His 1982 Davis Cup match with McEnroe began with a two hour first set. He lost in five sets. It was the first time France had reached the final in 49 years.*

LEFT: *Australians Mark Edmundson and Paul McNamee (on the left) shake hands with their conquerors John McEnroe and Peter Fleming in their 1984 semi-final. These two countries dominated the Davis Cup until the late 1970s.*

135

LEFT: *The victorious 1983 Australian Davis Cup team did not include one player in the world top 20.*

by a $1 million sponsorship deal with Nippon Electric Company (NEC), and the competition was restructured into two contests, one between the 16 top tennis nations, and the other a zonal battle for the remaining 40 or so entrants, the winners of each of the four zones earning a place among the top 16. This new format created some new and exciting ties, as nations now had to play anywhere in the world that the draw took them.

America, victors over Argentina in 1981, traveled to Grenoble the next year to play the French on their favorite surface: clay. The first set of McEnroe's match with Yannick Noah took nearly two hours, with the American eventually winning it 12-10. But the Frenchman fought back to take the next two sets, before the customary 15 minute break that the Davis Cup always has after a third set. McEnroe returned cool and ruthless, and pulled off the next two sets. He continued his brilliant form in the doubles, partnered by Peter Fleming against Noah and Leconte, and America won the tie.

Teenager Pat Cash was included in the team of Australians who surprisingly beat a very strong Swedish team (without Borg) in the 1983 final. It was the youngster's first year in the competition and he was nearly thrown out by his own captain for his irascible on-court behaviour.

Sweden was back in the 1984 final against the Americans and on a specially laid indoor clay court. McEnroe and Connors, two of the

best players in the world and, in theory, capable of carrying the tie on their own, did not overcome their mutual dislike and the team morale, so vital in the Davis Cup, was poor. The Americans only won one match. It was a performance made worse by some unsportsmanlike on-court activity from McEnroe and Connors. Sweden retained the trophy in a final with West Germany the next year, as the talents of Boris Becker were not enough to hold together the whole German team. In 1986 the powerful Swedes traveled to Melbourne to face Australia, and found Pat Cash and his colleagues invincible, winning his three rubbers to bring the trophy back down under.

In 1987, America continued its run of disastrous Davis Cup performances with a defeat by Paraguay, and subsequent relegation. Sweden comfortably took the cup again, beating India in the final.

Sweden reach its sixth consecutive final in 1988 and acted as hosts to West Germany, who behaved like the worst of guests by recovering from two sets down in both the opening matches and winning the tie to becoming the ninth nation with its name engraved on the trophy.

The countries listed in those last two paragraphs illustrate the role the Davis Cup plays in modern tennis. When nations such as Paraguay (albeit carried by one star player, Victor Pecci) can challenge the might of America, tennis can only benefit.

RIGHT: *McEnroe, Fleming, Noah and Leconte during a 1982 final when America beat France 4-1.*

Court's Grand Slam

At the public tennis park in Albury, Victoria, local children found a court which was half concealed from the beady eyes of the attendant. Provided they stayed mainly in one half of it, they could play for free. So one of the kids became highly adept at volleying every shot back at the net. Her name was Margaret Smith, and the volley she developed helped her to achieve a singles and, uniquely, a mixed doubles Grand Slam.

The athletic, hard hitting tomboy came under the wing of Frank Sedgman, and she was given grueling circuits to complete to build up her strength and stamina. She practised tennis two hours a day, and worked out in the gymnasium for three two-hour stints per week. In 1960, aged 17, she beat Maria Bueno and went on to win the Australian championship. After retaining the title the next year, she set off on a disastrous European tour where shrewd opponents remorselessly played to her main weakness, her forehand drive. By 1962 she was more tactically aware, and saved a match point against Lesley Turner in winning the French Open. Seeded number one for Wimbledon, an intimidated, nervous Court lost a 5-2 lead in the deciding set of her first match, to a precocious teenager called Billie Jean Moffitt.

1962 saw Court win the Australian, French and American championships to reach number one in the world rankings, and the following year she won three major titles again, gaining Wimbledon but dropping in the USA, where she suffered from not being able to practise on grass before the tournament. She did succeed in winning the first mixed doubles Grand Slam, with fellow Australian Kenneth Fletcher, however.

Margaret Court was a natural athlete, but a manufactured tennis player She needed lots of practice to keep her game at its peak, and although tall and powerful, she lacked confidence, sometimes suffering crippling nerves. Court continued a grueling rollercoaster of tournaments over the next few years, usually getting the better of her

The highs and lows of tennis.
ABOVE: *Margaret Court (then the 18-year-old Miss Smith) with her first Australian singles trophy, in 1960.*
RIGHT: *Looking rather weary during her 1969 Wimbledon semi-final defeat by Ann Jones. She bounced back next year with a 14-12, 11-9 finals victory over King.*

LEFT: *At nearly 5ft 9in (1.75m), Court had a great height advantage for her serve.*

RIGHT: *Rosie Casals, who succumbed to Court's relentless attack in the 1970 US Open final, which completed the Australian's Grand Slam.*

chief rivals Moffitt and Bueno, but the pleasure went out of tennis for her. She was on a nerve-grinding treadmill. She retired, and started running a boutique in Perth, marrying the well known yachtsman Barry Court the next year. Visiting friends with a tennis court, Court hit a few balls for fun . . . and caught the bug again. She prepared herself for a comeback.

It took a year to build up her technique and fitness, but by 1969, Court was back with a vengeance, winning every major title except Wimbledon. It was the last time she lost a Grand Slam event until May 1971.

1970 was a momentous year, for she won all four Grand Slam tournaments. In the Australian singles, she never dropped more than three games in a set. At the French Open, Olga Morozova and then Helga Hiessen put up more of a challenge, but the revitalized Court was able to hold her nerve. At Wimbledon, she met Billie Jean King in a fine match. Court had a blackened and swollen ankle but it held up through 148 minutes of fiercely competitive tennis, and she won the championship on her sixth match point. She hardly took a break before the American championships, perhaps to keep her mind off the importance of the tournament, and she lost only 13 games in the five matches it took to reach Rosie Casals in the final. That day the score read 6-2, 2-6, 6-1 and Court had completed her Grand Slam.

It was a hard act to follow, and although she won the Australian title in 1971, she failed in France and lost to Evonne Goolagong at Wimbledon. Margaret then left tennis for a year to have a child, returning to take three Grand Slam tournaments the next year (again missing out at Wimbledon, where her record is less impressive than elsewhere). Goolagong was twice her victim in the finals at Kooyong and in Paris, and she beat Evert in America. But Court could not hold back the new wave of women players and Evert and Navratilova became more than her match over the next few years.

She finally retired in 1977 with an impressive record over 16 years of tennis: 92 titles, including 67 in Grand Slam events. She won 11 Australian singles titles, five in France, three in Wimbledon, and seven American championships, plus the championships of Italy, Germany and South Africa. She also gathered the doubles at Wimbledon twice and the mixed five times, five US doubles and eight US mixed, four doubles and mixed titles in the French, and eight doubles and two mixed in Australia.

LEFT: *Court trained constantly to retain her match fitness and mental alertness. She had a strong on-court presence which intimidated opponents.*

Rocket

RIGHT: *Rod Laver at 21, showing the athleticism that helped him to achieve his Grand Slam . . .*

FAR RIGHT: *. . . collecting the Wimbledon trophy on the way to another Grand Slam in 1969.*

The first player to achieve two Grand Slams, and the first tennis millionaire, Rod Laver is rated by many in the sport as the best male tennis player the game has ever produced. His Grand Slams were separated by seven years, and had he not been a professional in the intervening period, he would certainly have picked up many more amateur titles.

Few would have predicted that Rod Laver would become a tennis great: small framed, slightly bandy legged, and quite puny in his youth, he hardly looked a winner. His father, a tennis enthusiast, groomed his older sons Trevor and Bob for tennis success on the clay court at home in Rockhampton, Queensland. But a coach called Charlie Hollis saw some potential in Rodney George, and he put the sunken chested youngster through a punishing training schedule to build up his strength. Rod Laver fulfilled his coach's faith by winning the Queensland under 14s championship, and three years later was introduced to the legendary Harry Hopman, Australia's Davis Cup coach. Laver impressed the great man with his sizzling service, and Hopman created a nickname that Laver lived up to: 'Rocket'.

Laver had the ingredients to be one of Hopman's success stories: mentally tough, a relentless attacker who hit the ball on the rise, fast, accurate, and wielding a vicious, swinging serve, decisive volleys, and accurate, sliced drives. He had to train hard to build stamina and strength, and was competing against some of the greatest players Australia had produced: Emerson, Fraser, Anderson, Cooper, Fletcher, Hoad and Rosewall.

BELOW: *The 1961 all-Australian US final, with Laver at the net and Roy Emerson, who won the match, racing for a return.*

RIGHT: *The Duke of Kent hands over the 1969 Wimbledon trophy, after watching Laver defeat John Newcombe.*

On a 1956 tour, aged 18, the red haired left-hander won the junior Wimbledon and US titles, and three years later had fought his way to play in the Davis Cup team against America. In 1960 he pulled back a two set deficit to beat Neale Fraser for the Australian title, but lost in the Wimbledon and US finals, although he retained his Wimbledon mixed title, paired with Darlene Hard. The next year he won his first Wimbledon singles in his third successive final, but lost to Emerson in the Australian and US championships.

The Grand Slam in 1962 began with a four set win over Emerson in Australia, and a grueling French championship in which he saved a match point against Martin Mulligan in the quarter finals, and then beat Emerson again in a draining final, 3-6, 2-6, 6-3, 9-7, 6-2. At Wimbledon he took only three sets to defeat Mulligan, and in the US finals it was, inevitably, Emerson he faced and conquered. Just for good measure Laver won the Italian and German titles that year, too.

Laver turned professional at the end of 1962, and won the US Pro title five times and the London title four times. In the first Open tournament, at Bournemouth in 1968, he lost to Ken Rosewall in the final, but the next year he achieved his second Grand Slam. This time, like Budge in 1938, he beat a different opponent in each final: the Spaniard Andres Gimeno in Australia, Rosewall in Paris, John Newcombe at Wimbledon, and Tony Roche at Forest Hills.

He was indisputably the top player in the world, amateur or professional. Perhaps that took some of the motivation out of his game, because he never won another Grand Slam title, although he did pass the £1 million earnings mark in 1971. His last notable win was in the 1973 Davis Cup final in Cleveland when he and Newcombe defeated America.

LEFT: *Laver was fast, clever, and left-handed – a formidable combination.*

Billie Jean

Billie Jean King became one of the legends of tennis because of the length and tenacity of her stay in the top class of the game. Billie Jean played to win. She also made a lasting impact on the politics of the game, promoting women's tennis to widespread acceptance both within and outside the tennis world.

Born Billie Jean Moffitt in November 1943 in Long Beach, California, she started playing tennis aged 11. She did not fit in with the stuffy country club atmosphere of US tennis, and from the age of 13 had the additional handicap of spectacles for her short sight. But King thrived on a challenge, and she always wanted to be the best tennis player in the world. Although she never won a junior title, she started to develop a fast, serve and volley game, helped by local coach Clyde Walker. She was also helped for a few months by the former champion Alice Marble, who built up her confidence.

Teamed with Karen Hantze for the doubles at Wimbledon in 1961, the young pair made a startling debut by winning the title, the first time an unseeded pairing had done so at Wimbledon. Chatty and approachable, King became an instant favorite with the Wimbledon crowd. In the singles, however, Yola Ramirez exploited her weak forehand and put her out although the next year King caused a sensation by knocking out Margaret Smith, the number one seed, in the first round.

Despite reaching the singles final at Wimbledon in 1963, King was aware that her game could be improved, and she was not devoting enough time to training because of her studies. This eventually led her to quit college and go to Australia in 1964 for training in technique and strokemaking from Mervyn Rose, a former Australian Davis Cup doubles player. She returned with a remodeled service and forehand, shorter backswing, and a much greater understanding of the game and of percentage play.

In 1966, King won her first Wimbledon singles title, defeating Maria Bueno. By 1979, she had achieved her twentieth Wimbledon title, surpassing Elizabeth Ryan's record. Her Wimbledon portfolio numbers ten doubles and four mixed titles, and she played her 265th and last game at the famous championships in 1983, losing the mixed doubles final. It was only the ninth time she had lost a Wimbledon final in 22 years. No wonder she said it was her favorite championship! King enjoyed a love-hate relationship with the Wimbledon public. Winning them over as a lively teenager, she began to meet hostility in the late 1960s as she continually won titles with her ruthless, determined play. By the end of her Wimbledon career, she was welcomed again as a familiar and much-loved face.

In her home country, King won 13 US championship titles, four

FAR LEFT: *Billie Jean King played aggressive, forceful tennis that made for some superb matches.*

ABOVE AND LEFT: *Always capable of surprising an opponent, King beat Evert in 1975 at the Wimbledon semi-finals, and went on to win her sixth singles title.*

singles, five doubles and four mixed, and she was the only woman to win US National titles on all four surfaces – grass, clay, hard and indoor. She also won titles in Australia, South Africa and many other countries: 39 Grand Slam titles in all, and in addition she had a pretty good record in the Wightman and Federation Cups. In 1971 she was the first woman to earn $100,000 from a year in tennis. It says much for her determination that King achieved these successes despite two knee operations, thyroid trouble, and the handicap of wearing spectacles.

In May 1981, King was sued for palimony by her ex-lover Marilyn Barnett, a hairdresser on the women's circuit. For the first time she publicly admitted to a lesbian affair and, with husband Larry a rock of support, bore the avalanche of publicity about her private life. She survived, won the palimony case, and continued to play tennis.

King earned a place in tennis history by fighting for the recognition of women's tennis: she was outspoken about the stupidity of shamateurism, and battled against the discrepancy in prize money between men's and women's tennis. She helped set up the womens pro circuit, and the Virginia Slim Grand Slam. She and her husband Larry King, who she married in 1965, organized and ran professional tournaments too. She also had the distinction of playing in the most publicized tennis event ever, the 1973 'Battle of the Sexes' against veteran professional Bobby Riggs. She took great pride in defeating him, believing she had won a battle for the credibility of women's tennis, as well as settling a few old scores with one of the critics of the women's game.

LEFT: *Never one to hide her emotions, King shows her anguish in her losing 1968 US final with Wade. Most of King's feelings about her private life have been forced into the public arena, too.*

RIGHT: *The 'Battle of the Sexes' in 1973, between Billie Jean King and Bobby Riggs, raised the profile of women's tennis. An articulate feminist, King made a massive contribution to the women's game.*

BELOW: *King combined with Navratilova to win the US doubles title in 1980.*

Borg the Invincible

RIGHT: *Spot the similarity: both sporting headbands, both reliant on heavy topspin, Borg and Vilas were at the pinnacle of tennis in the late 1970s. Borg twice beat the South American in French Open finals.*

BELOW AND RIGHT: *Borg's double-handed backhand (right) was rare at the time, and packed a vicious topspin. He relied on his groundstrokes, and his serve (below) did not match the power of many of his rivals. It didn't seem to matter.*

Bjorn Borg was, for several years, the best tennis player in the world, making up for a shaky volley and a weak second serve with a commitment and perseverance in match play that won him many titles, including five consecutive Wimbledon singles championships.

Always a reserved, enigmatic character, he retired from the game early, seemingly just too tired to carry on the slog of professional global tennis. In his wake he left a new enthusiasm for tennis in Sweden, memories of some great matches, mass hysteria among young girls, and a feeling that he had not put much back into the game that made him rich.

When Borg was nine his father, a leading table tennis player, won a tennis racket, and gave it to his son. The young Bjorn began to attack the garage wall with a vengeance, and tennis joined his other sporting obsession, ice hockey. Gladly leaving school early at the age of 15, Borg immediately won a junior tournament in Florida, following that up in 1972 with a win over Buster Mottram in the Junior Wimbledon competition.

When he joined Sweden's Davis Cup team, Borg came into contact with the team coach and captain, Lennart Bergelin, who later became his manager. During the Davis Cup training period, the young Borg's temper tantrums infuriated Bergelin, who hurled a racket at the newcomer's head. Thus was born the famous cool, controled Borg temperament.

In 1974 Borg was the youngest player ever to win the Italian championship, taking the scalps of Orantes, Vilas and Nastase. The next week he won the French Open, this time beating Raul Ramirez, Harold Solomon, and Orantes again in the final, where he recovered from being two sets down. Significantly for the future, he also won a grass tournament, the New Zealand Open. By the close of the year Borg was ranked third in the world, the endorsement contracts were rolling in, and, with his long blond hair kept in place by a headband, he was the teenybopper's idol. He opted for tax exile in Monte Carlo in 1975. The disapproval of the Swedish press was tempered by his invaluable performances in the Davis Cup which helped Sweden win the trophy for the first time.

Borg's play centered on his groundstrokes. He whipped up vicious topspin forehand drives, and his double-handed backhand was unerring. It was a game of patience and consistency, with the simple aim of hitting one more shot than his opponent. His rackets were strung extremely tightly and he frequently broke the strings, once getting through 28 in six days, so batches of rackets were air freighted around the world from his stringer in Stockholm. The distinctive ping of a string breaking sometimes woke up Bergelin in his hotel room in the middle of the night.

Borg's style was ideally suited to slow, clay courts, and for six years he was just about unbeatable on the surface, winning six French singles titles, two Italian championships, and three US Pro championships. At Forest Hills in the US Open, he could not cope with the floodlights, high bounces and firm footholds of the concrete courts, and lost four finals, twice each to Connors and McEnroe.

Remarkably, however, Borg gathered five successive Wimbledon singles titles, despite the fast grass surface and the fact that players have only two weeks to adjust from the slow clay of the French Open. He always enjoyed playing at Wimbledon, and relied on his superb passing shots to make up for a mediocre volley.

In 1976, Borg's opponent in the final was Ilie Nastase, and the Romanian's artistry could not challenge the pounding drives from the Swede, who won in three sets, having nervously lost the first three games. The next year he won an exhausting five set semi-final against his friend Vitas Gerulaitis and was still suffering the after effects as he faced Jimmy Connors in the final. For three and a half hours the American and the Swede battled, both playing mainly from the baseline. Connors fought back from 0-4 down in the final set to reach level terms, but found that it is easier to take risks when playing from behind, and lost the next two games and the match.

They met again in the 1978 final, and this time Borg steamrollered through the match in three sets, playing formidably powerful tennis. Borg enjoyed attacking the Connors serve. The next year he faced the fastest server in the game, Roscoe Tanner. The American had a two sets to one lead, but Borg showed his determination to return that cannonball service and forced errors from Tanner at the net. Borg's mother was eating candy for luck during the match. When he had three match points at 5-4, 40-0, in the fifth set, she spat it out. Tanner fought back to deuce. Mrs Borg retrieved the candy from the floor, put it in her mouth, and her son won the next two points and the match!

The 1980 final was one of the greatest ever, a thrilling five set marathon of almost four hours against the precocious John McEnroe. Both men showed phenomenal athleticism in reaching seemingly lost balls and producing winning strokes. The see-sawing match culminated with a tie break in the fourth set which lasted an emotionally grueling 20 minutes. First Borg had a series of match points, then McEnroe's daring return earned him some set points, and he clinched it as Borg missed a forehand volley. In the final set, Borg's serve clicked into place, and McEnroe won only three points off it. It was his 35th consecutive win at Wimbledon, probably the hardest, and certainly the pinnacle of his career.

McEnroe won the return match the next year, and from fall 1981 the great Swede played only lucrative exhibitions and special events. He seemed worn out by the grind of constant traveling, and the concentration needed to play the game his way. Two attempted comebacks, in 1982 and 1984, came to nothing, and eventually his marriage to Marianna Simionescu fell apart, too. Perhaps the strain of playing error free, accurate tennis while maintaining the coolest temperament in the game was just too heavy for a man who had made enough money to retire comfortably in his mid-twenties.

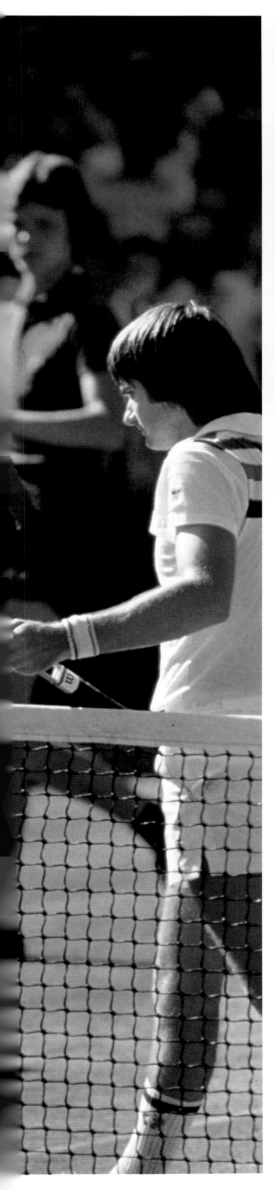

TOP LEFT: *Borg after his first Wimbledon win, in straight sets over Nastase in 1976 . . . and (center) the next year, after a much tougher five-setter against Connors.*

ABOVE: *Borg disliked the concrete courts at Flushing Meadow, and the floodlights that always lit the final. Consequently, he lost four titles there.*

RIGHT: *Borg prepares to serve during his epic Wimbledon final against John McEnroe in 1980.*

Jimbo the Fighter

RIGHT AND BELOW: *Years of triumph for Connors: brandishing the US Open trophy after decimating Rosewall in 1974, and (above) belting a typical double-handed backhand in 1982 on his way to beating Lendl in New York.*

FAR RIGHT: *Connors has never won the French Open title; here he summons up concentration during the 1985 tournament.*

Jimmy Connors is a fighter. Since 1971, tennis fans have adored watching Jimbo slug out a rally, belt a double-backhand winner, turn and pound his thighs in exhortation for the next point. Often a controversial figure, he has gathered more than 100 major titles in a career that has seen many ups and a few downs.

Born in East St Louis in 1952, Connors was always very close to Gloria, his mother, and his grandmother (known as 'Two Mom'), who acted together as his coach, manager and adviser. They tutored him on the court at the back of the house for which Gloria herself had cleared the land. Here the left-handed Connors started to develop a punishingly accurate double-handed backhand, which spearheaded a fast and furious baseline game where the balls were hit early and flat. His game was refined in California by Pancho Gonzales and Segura, and at 20 he won his first pro title in Jacksonville, and reached the last 16 at Wimbledon, where he was beaten by future doubles partner Nastase (they were to win Wimbledon in 1973 and the US Open in 1975). The next year he won the US Pro and Jimmy was on his way.

1974 was a remarkable year for Connors. Winning 99 out of 103 matches, he won Wimbledon, the US and Australian Opens with brutally powerful tennis, and reached number one in the rankings – he was not out of the top three for the next 12 years. The Australian and Wimbledon wins were both over the veteran Rosewall, 19 years older and unable to cope with the sustained aggression of Connors' game. It seemed he would reign at the top for some time.

In 1975, however, he reached the same three finals, and lost them all. Most significant was the way Arthur Ashe beat him at Wimbledon, depriving him of the pace his game fed on and unsettling him with angled, chipped and floated shots. Great competitor that he was, Jimbo just couldn't find the answer.

Over the next three years, he managed major wins in the US Open (1976, on clay), the WCT Masters (1977, against Dick Stockton), and the US Open again (1978, on cement against Borg who had beaten him in the Wimbledon final). But much of the time his spark and bravado were gone, and he lost innumerable semi-final matches.

LEFT: *At 33, Connors still showed the fierce determination that took him to the top.*

BELOW LEFT: *A familiar sight to many tennis fans: Connors sprinting along the baseline to thump back another flat drive.*

MAIN PICTURE: *Connors is a volatile character, capable of hilarious clowning one minute, and boorish berating of officials the next.*

It was 1982 before he won another top title. In the intervening years he showed patchy form, and agreed to represent the US in the Davis Cup for the first time since 1975. He and McEnroe behaved so badly in their tie that they were close to being banned from representing the US again. Throughout his career Connors proved capable of some highly offensive behaviour on court, swearing, gesticulating, and intimidating line judges – although he delighted crowds with flashes of humor and irreverence.

In 1982 Connors returned to form, and in a vintage year beat McEnroe (who was now ranked number one) at Wimbledon and Lendl in the US Open. He retained his US title the following year, and in 1984 was runner up to McEnroe at Wimbledon. That year he also teamed up with his erstwhile fiancé, Chris Evert, to win the World Mixed Doubles Championship.

Another barren patch was lifted by the spirited tennis Connors played in 1987, qualifying for the Masters for a record eleventh time, reaching three finals, and making a magnificent recovery from 1-6, 1-6, 1-4 against Mikael Pernfors in the quarter-final at Wimbledon. The next year two operations on his feet gave some indication of the battering they had taken over his career, and although Connors remains as competitive as ever, the task of winning another grand slam title is getting harder.

At his worst a strutting, blustering bully, at his best a courageous and exciting competitor, Connors truly made his mark in tennis, mostly with sheer guts and determination. He remains a player his fellow professionals fear on court; throughout his career his pride has made him fight to the last point, winning him some remarkable victories.

McEnroe the Volatile Genius

Superbrat, McEnrow, The Incredible Sulk: the nicknames and headlines given to John McEnroe in his career tell their own story of the controversy he generated among players, officials and spectators alike. But setting aside the vagaries of his temperamental behavior, he stands as the most talented, exciting player ever to wield a tennis racket. He also held the number one spot in the world for four years after the demise of Borg, at a time when the standard of men's play had never been better.

Born on a US airbase in West Germany in 1959, but soon moving to the family home in New York, McEnroe started playing tennis at a local club when he was eight. He was a Forest Hills ballboy many times, and had a natural affinity with the game. When he was 12, he was challenged by a boy four years older to a match, and given a 5-0 head start in each set. He won comfortably against his giant opponent, who was Peter Fleming, his future friend and doubles partner.

McEnroe exploded on to the tennis scene in 1977. Having captured the French mixed doubles title with Mary Carillo, he won through the qualifying rounds for Wimbledon, and the precocious teenager got as far as the semi-finals, where Jimmy Connors stopped him.

Sensibly advised by his family to continue his college studies for at least another year, McEnroe won the NCAA as a Stanford freshman in 1978, and then turned professional. His playing bemused even the most experienced opponents. A left hander, his serve carried a vicious slice, or could go like lightning down the center line. It was backed by probably the best second serve in the game. But once a rally began, McEnroe was a supreme improviser, using his quick reflexes to switch shots at the last moment. His angled drives and volleys, cunning disguised lobs and delicate touch that allowed him to

ABOVE AND LEFT: *Two faces of McEnroe. Left, the intense concentration as he delivers a delicate shot, and above, during one of his child-like encounters with authority.*

RIGHT: *McEnroe's serve carries a vicious slice, taking it right off the court. Occasionally he blasts a cannonball down the middle, just for variety. He had to adapt the stroke as its twisting delivery gave him back trouble.*

punch or kill the ball, all helped him to keep the ball out of reach of his opponent. It was a total contrast to the mechanical, patient Borg.

Yet his volatile Irish-American temperament made McEnroe a moody player. His perfectionist approach to the game turned frustration at his mistakes into deepest gloom, and his arrogant outbursts when he did not agree with line calls or official rulings were a

LEFT: *McEnroe's flexible wrist is capable of returning the ball at astonishing angles.*

RIGHT: *Peter Fleming and John McEnroe formed a superb doubles team, taking Wimbledon in 1979, 1981, 1983 and 1984, the US Open in 1979, 1981 and 1983, the Masters from 1978-1984, and the World Doubles in 1979.*

BELOW: *With his Wimbledon trophy of 1981. Note the Davis Cup top: McEnroe sacrificed time and money to play for his country at a time when some of his contemporaries chose not to.*

sickening spectacle on the court. Ironically, while infuriating every-body else (including his becalmed opponent), these battles often motivated McEnroe to his best tennis. McEnroe was a lazy trainer, preferring to hone his skills in doubles play rather than spend hours on the practice courts. His lack of regular training could explain the frequent breaks in his career caused by injury.

In 1978 he saved two match points against Arthur Ashe to take the Masters title, and the following year he beat Gerulaitis for the US Open. He was to hold the title for three successive years, for in the next two finals he frustrated the great Borg.

In the third year of winning, McEnroe became the first man to be ranked number one in both singles and doubles lists. Paired with the consistent Fleming, McEnroe's incisive volleys made for a superb doubles combination, and together they won numerous titles.

At Wimbledon, McEnroe reached five single finals in a row. In the first in 1980, he lost to Borg in a thrilling match but got his revenge the next year, winning two tie breakers in a four sets victory to take the title. But once again controversy ruled as the All England Club decided that his behavior during the tournament barred him from the traditional honor of club membership. It was just one of many wars with authority in his career.

The 1982 Wimbledon final against Jimmy Connors was a long, temperamental match which did not endear him any more to the Wimbledon crowd, and he lost in five sets. However over the next two years he scored easy wins over Chris Lewis, and then Connors. He was finally accepted for membership of the famous Club.

In this year he also helped his country win the Davis Cup, as he had done in 1978, 1979, and 1981. McEnroe's eagerness to play in Davis Cup matches for America helped to revive a competition which was becoming second rate, and his willingness to make the financial sacrifices involved in playing Davis Cup (missing lucrative tournaments and exhibition matches) contrasts with many of his fellow countrymen. McEnroe continued as the world number one until 1985, beating Lendl for the US Open crown the previous year.

Marriage and fatherhood seemed to have calmed that volcano-like temperament, but, perhaps because of this, McEnroe did not win a major title after 1985. Surprisingly, he never won a tournament played on clay – apart from the French junior in 1977 – but his record of four US Opens and WCT titles, and three Wimbledon and Masters wins, plus countless doubles championships, ensures his place in tennis history as one of the greats.

Leading by Example

In November 1970, weeks after Margaret Court had achieved her Grand Slam, she was beaten 7-6, 7-6 at a tournament in Charlotte, North Carolina by a 15-year-old American girl called Chris Evert. The next year Evert notched up 46 consecutive singles wins before losing to Billie Jean King in the semi-finals of the US Championships, and became the youngest player ever to represent the United States, demolishing Wade 6-1, 6-1 as her country won the Wightman Cup.

It was quite a way to arrive on the tennis scene, but the equable teenager seemed to take it all in her stride. Born in Fort Lauderdale, Florida, just before Christmas in 1954, Evert was conditioned from an early age to work at her tennis by her father Jimmy who was a teaching pro. From the age of six, he taught her that winners are the players who make the least errors, and that you should never reveal your feelings to your opponent.

When she started playing tennis, Evert was not strong enough to hold the racket properly on her backhand, and so was born the famous double-handed stroke that became her trademark. Like Maureen Connolly, she stayed on the baseline nearly all the time, thumping back well-placed drives interspersed with the occasional drop shot, and attacking volleyers with lobs and accurate passing shots.

Her cool concentration on court earned her nicknames such as 'The Ice Queen', but she was a popular player because of her graceful femininity and sense of humor. Part of the secret of her long, successful career was that although she was pushed from an early age, she did not turn professional until she was 18 – until then, she took her homework to every tournament she played. When she was able to take prize money, her father formed a corporation to invest the winnings. By 1988, she had won $8,664,510.

Moments from a distinguished career. LEFT: *After beating Court 6-1, 1-6, 6-1 in the 1973 Wimbledon semi-final.* ABOVE: *Engaged Wimbledon champions Evert and Connors made a glamorous couple in 1974.* TOP: *With the youngster who* *copied her style and beat her, Tracy Austin.*

RIGHT: *The double-handed backhand that thousands copied, still smooth in 1989 at the US Open, where she announced her retirement.*

After two years of almost winning titles, 1974 was a glory year for Evert. She went 56 matches without loss to take ten tournaments, including Rome, Paris and Wimbledon, beating Navratilova in Italy and twice trouncing Morozova for the other titles. At Forest Hills, her loss to Goolagong, was to be her last US Open defeat for five years, and she won at least one Grand Slam title over the next 13 years.

1974 was also the year of her much publicized engagement to Jimmy Connors who was blazing his own trail in men's tennis. They shared titles honors at Wimbledon that year, bringing a touch of romance to the Wimbledon Ball at which the singles champions share the first dance. The day before the wedding invitations were to be issued they decided not to marry, but they remain good friends.

From 1975 to 1978 Evert was number one in the world. For those four full years she won every US Open, took the French (1975) and Wimbledon (1976). She lost two Wimbledon finals in 1978 and 1979 to Navratilova, who has dogged her throughout her career. Evert was particularly welcomed by the Wimbledon crowd in 1979 as she had recently married British player John Lloyd, forming the most glamorous couple in tennis. It was not an easy marriage, beset by the problems of two busy worldwide playing schedules, and they eventually divorced in 1987.

LEFT: *The victory gesture doesn't celebrate any old win: this was Evert after defeating Navratilova for the first time in 13 attempts, in the 1985 Virginia Slims finals.*

ABOVE: *(inset) Evert and Navratilova's friendship and rivalry were the motifs of women's tennis in the 1980s.*

ABOVE: *Evert looks uncomfortable stretching for a ball halfway up the court. Her natural role is to roam the baseline, firing off superbly placed drives.*

In 1979 she lost her six year dominance on the clay of the Italian Open, to the young Tracy Austin. Ironically Austin aped Evert's patient baseline game and double handed backhand better than anyone, and repeated her win in the US Open the same year. Twelve months later Evert defeated the young pretender in the semi-final at Flushing Meadow, recovering from a 4-0 deficit in the first set by varying her shots and exploiting Austin's lack of flexibility. It was the year that saw her fight back to regain her top ranking with eight tournament wins, including the Italian and French Opens. Again there was disappointment at Wimbledon as she surprisingly lost the final to a revitalized Evonne Cawley.

But in 1981, at last, Evert gathered her third Wimbledon title, without dropping a set in the tournament, and beating the Czech Mandlikova – who had knocked out Evert's main threat, Navratilova – 6-2, 6-2 in the semi-final. It was sweet revenge, as the erratic Czech girl had beaten her for the French Open title in the same year.

Evert continued to win major titles over the next few years, but started to lose regularly to the much improved and determined Navratilova. In 1984, for example, she was runner up to the Czech defector at Paris, Wimbledon and Flushing Meadow. However, on her best surface, clay, she defeated Navratilova in the French finals of 1985 and 1986, achieving a record of seven French Open championships.

1987 was a disappointing year beset by injuries and her divorce, and she dropped a place in the rankings. She beat her long standing rival and friend to reach the Australian finals in 1988, which she lost, and with the emergence of Graf, the power axis in women's tennis shifted. She announced before the 1989 US Open that it would be her last major tournament, and made a tearful exit in the quarter-finals as she lost to Zina Garrison.

Evert's career helped to shape women's tennis. Countless youngsters have been encouraged into the game by her skills and demeanour, and her duel for top prizes with Martina Navratilova helped sustain interest in the women's game and raised the standard so that others, such as Graf, had to match it.

Scaling New Heights

Martina Navratilova set out to be the greatest tennis player of all time. Her dedication to this aim led her to desert her homeland and family, and to use every tool and person available to improve her game. The highest earning tennis player so far (by 1988 her career prize money alone was more than $14 million) she has won numerous major titles and two Grand Slams.

A small scrawny child born on the outskirts of Prague, she was tennis mad and in 1965 still a tiny nine-year-old when she won an under-12s tournament. Only eight years later and already Czech champion, Martina created a stir in the 1973 French Open by beating Nancy Richey, a past winner, but lost to Goolagong in the quarter-finals.

Having led Czechoslovakia to the Federation Cup title in 1975, Navratilova made the momentous decision to defect, asking for asylum in America the day after she lost, to Evert, in the US Open. Although her family were tacitly aware that she found life in Czechoslovakia restrictive, the 18-year-old was not able to say goodbye before she left as it would incriminate them. The constant supplies of food and other luxuries of life in the States, caused Navratilova to balloon in weight and her tennis suffered – in the 1976 US Open she lost in the first round. Golf professional Sandra Haynie (the first of a number of advisers) improved her match tactics and made her diet. Six tournament wins in 1977 showed the decline had stopped.

She began 1978 with a run of 37 consecutive wins, and she finally broke Evert's four year domination of women's tennis by beating her 2-6, 6-4, 7-5 in the Wimbledon final and winning the women's num-

ber one ranking. The following year she repeated the feat in the final, and won ten other tournaments as well, although her tennis was overshadowed to a certain extent by family events. Her whole family came to live in Dallas. But her stepfather, who had always been close to her, could not adjust to life in the States, or accept his daughter's bisexuality, and in June 1980 they went back to Prague.

Navratilova slumped and did not win a major tournament in 1980, losing to Evert in the Wimbledon semi-final, and to fellow Czech Mandlikova in the US Open. At 24, she faced a crisis: she had stopped caring if she lost, and her motivation was gone. Her rescuer this time was basketball star Nancy Lieberman, who forced her into a regime of fitness training that few tennis players could manage.

Navratilova really wanted to win the US Open: she had finally obtained her passport and become an American citizen, and it was now her national championship. A record crowd of 18,892 saw her demolish Austin in the first set 6-1, but then she lost two tie breaks and the match. Watching her every move was Renée Richards, who spotted her technical errors, and became her coach right after the match. Renée Richards had become something of a cause célèbre in tennis because she was born a man, Richard Raskind, and had a sex change. She fought a battle with the authorities and the media to be accepted as a female player.

Under Richard's guidance, the former Czech became an invincible player, winning six successive Wimbledons and many other

major titles. Now she prepared for every match not just physically but mentally and tactically, studying her opponent's weaknesses and exploiting them. Already a powerful left-hander with an excellent serve and superb volleys, Navratilova acquired several new strokes and became supreme in all aspects of the game.

In 1982, Martina won all but three of her 93 matches, picking up the French and Wimbledon titles in the process. She also helped the USA to win the Federation Cup with a 3-0 win over Germany at Santa Clara, the first player to compete in the competition for more than one country. She finally won the US Open title that had eluded her for so long in 1983, beating, appropriately enough, Evert in straight sets. Navratilova was in intimidating form and no one had kept her on court more than an hour in the championship so far. Her new coach Mike Estep advised her to force Evert into going for her winners by charging the net. She won the first set in 25 minutes, and clinched the match on her fourth match point, after 63 minutes on court.

In 1984 she set a record of 74 straight wins and achieved the Grand Slam (although she did not win all four titles in the calendar year – a Grand Slam can now be achieved in any 12 month period). The feat earned her a bonus of £1 million from the International Tennis Federation. The next year her unbeaten streak of 109 doubles matches with partner Pam Shriver came to an end. Navratilova always enjoyed playing doubles (she partnered Evert for a while) and believes it provides valuable match practice. She and Shriver won 19 major doubles titles together.

Navratilova won at least one major title every year up to and including 1987, by which time Graf had taken up number one spot in the rankings, despite the fact that Navratilova beat her to equal Helen Wills' record of eight Wimbledon singles wins. Graf showed her supremacy by beating her in the 1988 and 1989 Wimbledon finals, and in the 1989 US Open decider when Navratilova, a set and 4-2 up, seemed to lose mental strength and double faulted twice to give the German the break back.

Navratilova's 48 Grand Slam titles have only been bettered by Court, and she has equalled Court's feat of winning singles and doubles Grand Slams, while she also matched King's 1973 triple crown in the US Open ten years later. Her aggressive play scaled new heights in women's tennis, but she was unable to fight off her young pretender.

FAR LEFT: *Intensive training and the use of the latest gymnasium technology enabled Navratilova to retain her on-court speed.*

ABOVE: *Accepting the applause of the Wimbledon crowd in 1988, by which time she had set new standards in the game.*

LEFT: *Navratilova congratulates Steffi Graf who beat her at Wimbledon in 1988 and 1989.*

Champions from Germany

In the 1980s two startling young talents emerged from West Germany to storm the tennis world. Boris Becker and, more particularly, Steffi Graf have made a massive impact on the game, and their youth and potential to improve must be worrying their opponents the world over.

Graf joined the elite of tennis history in 1988, before she was 20. Her 'Golden Slam' – all four Grand Slam titles and a gold medal in the Seoul Olympics – established her as by far the best woman player in the world. She almost repeated her Grand Slam the next year, but was frustrated by a shock loss in the French Open. She still lives with her family in the town where she was born, Bruehl, in West Germany. From the age of four, her father Peter encouraged her to practice against a wall with rewards of lollipops.

In 1982, at 13 years of age, Graf became the youngest ever player to earn a ranking place from the Women's International Tennis Association, and in 1984 she reached the quarter-finals of Wimbledon. The next year she progressed to the last 16 at Paris and Wimbledon, and the semi-finals of the US Open, and in 1986 won her first pro tournament beating Evert in the Hilton Head final. She went on to defeat Navratilova for the German Open title, lost to Mandlikova in the French quarter finals, and a virus prevented her entering Wimbledon. In the US Open, Graf lost a semi-final battle with Navratilova having had three match points, but could console herself that she won eight of the 11 tournaments she entered in 1986 – and clearly, her play could improve.

A week before her eighteenth birthday, Graf won her first Grand Slam title when she took the French Open, beating Navratilova 6-4, 4-6, 8-6 in a tough final. At Wimbledon they met again, but on grass the powerful Navratilova was too strong for the German and a run of 45 matches without defeat was ended. The result was the same at the US Open, but by then Graf was ranked number one after she beat Evert to win the Virginia Slim championship.

1988 was a golden year for the German tennis star, as she became only the sixth player ever to achieve a singles Grand Slam, putting herself next to Don Budge, Maureen Connolly, Rod Laver, Margaret Court and Martina Navratilova in the history books. Seeded first at every tournament, she won each of them with confident, assured play that belied the pressure she was under. In Australia, Evert became her victim in two sets, the second on a tie break. At the French, Graf humiliated Natalia Zvereva of the Soviet Union 6-0, 6-0. She looked in trouble in the Wimbledon final, 5-7 and 0-2 down against Navratilova, but bounced back to take 12 of the next 13 games. Her forehands had never been harder, her service was impossible to anticipate. At the US Open, she faced possibly her nearest rival, Gabriela Sabatini, and took three sets to clinch the title.

BELOW LEFT: *The scoreboard tells the story of Graf's 1989 Wimbledon revenge over her French Open conqueror, Arantxa Sanchez.*

BELOW RIGHT: *Fast on her long legs, and possessed of an array of textbook shots, Graf looks set to dominate the 1990s.*

ABOVE RIGHT: *Graf (right) with Navratilova after the Czech-born player had won Wimbledon 1987.*

FAR RIGHT: *Graf with fellow German Boris Becker, winners of Wimbledon 1989.*

BELOW RIGHT: *Graf delivers a crushing forehand drive.*

She embellished the achievement with a gold medal in the Seoul Olympics. In 1988, Graf lost only three of her 75 matches, the victors being Sabatini (twice) and Shriver, with two of the losses following a bout of 'flu and a six-week break from the game.

The question on everyone's lips was whether she could do it again. Taking the Australian Open, she seemed full of confidence, but in Paris she was upset in the final by the precocious and flamboyant Arantxa Sanchez. She recovered to take the Wimbledon title with a ruthless win over Navratilova, and in a repeat performance took the US Open in a match where she gave her opponent a few chances but stepped up a gear to take the third set 6-1.

Graf has begun a new era in women's tennis, both in seeing off the arch rivals Evert and Navratilova, and in her athletic, all court game. Her serve is scorching and difficult to read, her volleys are precise, and her sliced backhand is highly consistent. But the most formidable weapon in her armory is the driven forehand, the most feared shot in the women's game, hit with a whip of the wrist that propels the ball harder than anyone else on the circuit. Her long legs give her superb mobility about the court, and overall she is a natural athlete. She sets the standard for the next breed of players to beat.

Boris Becker was the first unseeded player to win the Wimbledon men's title, and the youngest ever champion at 17 years and 7 months in 1985. It was an amazing entry into top tennis, even given his previous achievements of reaching the last 16 in the 1984 Australian Open, and winning both the inaugural World Young Masters for under 21s and the Queens tournament prior to Wimbledon.

How did he do it? First, his powerful service is best suited to grass, and the surface also allows him to land safely from the athletic leaps he makes for balls that ought to be ought of reach. Second, even at 17 he was a mature, confident and determined player who could cope with the pressures of match play.

His first coach, Romanian Gunther Bosch, detected the look of a

LEFT: *Becker's rampaging and powerful style has few margins for error.*

ABOVE: *Becker will chase every ball, whether he lands on the ground or in the net.*

ABOVE RIGHT: *A characteristic gesture as Becker gets charged up for a key point.*

winner in Becker when he was an overweight, temperamental nine year old with steely, alert eyes. Bosch developed the youngster's aggressive game, and in 1982 he won the first of three successive German National Junior Championships.

That astonishing first Wimbledon was followed by something even more remarkable: coping with the pressure of being the title holder. Still only 18, Becker destroyed Lendl in three sets to retain the championship in 1986.

1987 was a bad year for Becker, as he quarreled with Bosch and severed the relationship, rebeling against his coach's insistence on being with him all the time. Then, an inspired Peter Doohan knocked him out of Wimbledon in the second round, and a knee injury put him out of tennis for six months. His career had received some blows as shattering as his own blasts of the ball. But a switch to a new coach, Bob Brett of Australia, and rest, repaired the damage, and after being thwarted by Edberg in the 1988 Wimbledon final, he produced a brilliant performance in the US Masters to unseat Lendl in a thrilling five-set final. Shortly afterwards he led Germany to its first ever Davis Cup victory in the final against Sweden. Boris was back in form.

At Wimbledon in 1989 he blasted his way to the final and easily beat a subdued Edberg to collect his third men's championship, still only 21. That year he also won his first major title away from the grass of the All England Club, beating Lendl to take the US Open title. The win established him as one of the truly great players of the current game. Since the last war, only a few men have won the Wimbledon and US titles in the same year: Laver, Connors, McEnroe, and now Becker.

Becker has improved his groundstrokes and his on-court speed and mobility in recent years. Although he has suffered a number of injury problems, when his smooth, ruthless machinery is running well, he looks invincible on fast surfaces.

The Future

The balance of power in tennis is changing, as a new generation of top players emerges from countries who have not previously produced champions, and as the game's internal politics develop.

On the talent side, a new breed of European players arrived in the 1980s, sweeping out the old guard of Americans and Australians. Many current top players – Edberg, Becker, Mecir, Wilander – are European, and there are few Americans to match them. In the women's game, Graf leads the way, but the explosive arrival of Sanchez of Spain to win the 1989 French Open gives hope of a challenge from another European country.

America and, most recently, Australia both have excellent junior coaching schemes which will help develop talent, but one of the greatest spurs to future players is a new hero. Chris Evert inspired thousands of young American girls to take up tennis – because she was poised, elegant, feminine, and made tennis an attractive sport. Bjorn Borg had a similar effect on young Swedes – and Scandinavia is now reaping the reward of his efforts as Edberg, Wilander, Jarrad reach their peak years. The West German duo of Becker and Graf, now joined by the exciting talent of Carl-Uwe Steel, an ex-decathlete, will undoubtedly encourage the youngsters of Hamburg and Berlin to take up the game, and if Sanchez continues to take the limelight, with fellow national Conchita Martinez following her, Spanish children will no doubt be inspired, too.

As the ebb and flow of veterans and young pretenders continues, America has high hopes for male players such as Chang, Agassi, Pete Sampras and Jim Courier, while Argentina's Alberto Mancini is also tipped for a long stay at the top. In the women's game, Yugoslavia's Monica Seles and Americans Jennifier Capriati and Mary Joe Fernandez togeher with Canada's Helen Kelesi, Czech Jana Novotna, and Natalia Zvereva from the USSR, will try to knock the remarkable Graf off her perch.

All these players are entering a pressure chamber which churns out casualties at an alarming rate. Mental burn out certainly contributed to the demise of Tracy Austin and Andrea Jaeger, and today many players are rarely seen without an injury-quelling bandage strapped on to a damaged limb. The controversial decision to introduce drug testing in 1990 implies that some players have chosen artificial methods of improving their performances – something which will not be tolerated.

One of the major new influences on tennis is its presence at the Olympics, which lends a new kudos to the game, and will stir many nations to search for and cultivate tennis talent. From 1990, the ATP is to run the men's tournament circuit, intending to cut back on the number of events to increase the quality of tournaments and give players a chance of a break from the game. During the negotiations for this switch, however, the ATP trod on a number of toes, and there is still much bridge building to be done before the game can truly present that important unified front to the world.

OPPOSITE PAGE: *Five years separated these moments. On the left, 15-year-old Stefan Edberg clutches the Wimbledon junior champion's trophy in 1983. On the right, after his 1988 triumph. Edberg is different from many other Swedish players because he prefers fast surfaces, and uses a single-grip backhand.*

LEFT: *Jennifer Capriati: will this teenage newcomer knock Graf off her perch?*

BELOW LEFT: *Michael Chang looked even younger than his 17 years during his 1989 French Open win.*

BELOW: *Andrea Jaeger, a young hope in the early 1980s, she lost interest in competitive tennis, burned out by the pressure.*

ACKNOWLEDGMENTS

The author would like to thank his wife Emma for her help and support during the composition of this book.

The Publishers would like to thank Judith Millidge, the Editor Moira Dykes, the Picture Researcher, Mike Rose the Designer and Emma Callery who compiled the index. We would also like to thank the following agencies and institutions for supplying the illustrations on the pages noted below:

Aberdeen Art Gallery and Museums page 9.
Courtesy of Adidas (UK) Ltd. (photo Peter Fletcher) page 104 below.
Allsport pages 2-3, 37 below, 54 right, 63 below, 78, 101, 102, top, 103, 110 top left and bottom two, 111 top, 113 both right, 115 below, 117, 119 top, 120 below, 121 top, 122 top right, 125 both, 126 both, 127, 128 right, 129, 130 both, 132 both, 133 both, 135 top, 136 both, 138, 139 both, 141, 145 bottom two, 148 top, 149, 150 both, 151 below, 155, 159 top, 160 top right, 163 inset, 164 top, 165, 167 both, 169 all three, 170, 171 right, 172 both, 173 bottom two.
Australian Overseas Information Service, London pages 86 top, 92 center, 120 top, 137 top.
The Bettmann Archive page 22 below.
Courtesey Dunlop-Slazenger page 106 top two.
Courtesy of the Richard Green Gallery, London page 12 top.
Hulton-Deutsch Collection pages 10 below, 12 below, 17 below, 22 top, 24 top, 27, 36 right, 66-67, 75, 77, 79 both, 80 top, 81 top, 82 top, 84 top, 87 top, 88 below, 89 both, 90, 92 top and below, 94, 95 bottom right, 97 both, 99 top, 104 top, 105 both, 108 top, 109 all three, 112 both, 112-113, 114 top right, 121 below, 122 below, 134 top, 137 below, 143 both, 144, 145, top, 154, below, 159 below.
Illustrated London News Picture Library pages 17 top, 26-27, 30 right, 35 below, 43 right, 46 below, 48 top, 51 all three, 62 all three, 63 top, 81 below, 83.
International Tennis Hall of Fame and Tennis Museum at the Newport Casino, Newport, Rhode Island, page 24 both.
The London Transport Museum page 34 center.
The Mansell Collection page 18 left, 19 below, 52 top.
Peter Newark's Historical Pictures pages 10 top, 11 right, 13, 14 below, 15 both, 20, 25 left, 30 below.
Copyright Carol L Newsom pages 6, 102 below, 106 bottom two, 107, 110 top right, 111 below, 113 top left, 118 below, 119 below, 122 top left, 123, 124, 128 left and below, 131 both, 147 below, 148 below, 151 top, 157, 158, 161, 162-163, 166, 168 both, 171 left, 173 top, 174.
Reuters/Bettmann Newsphotos page 140.
UPI/Bettmann Newsphotos pages 1, 23 right, 31, 36 left, 38 both, 39 both, 40 all three, 41 both, 42, 43 top and left, 44-45 all three, 46 top, 56, 57 top, 58 both, 59 top, 64, 65 top, 68-69 all three, 72-73 all five, 76 both, 81 below, 82 below, 84 below, 85 both, 86 below, 87 below, 88 top, 91 both, 93, 94-95, 95 top right and left, 96, 98 both, 99 below, 114 left and below, 115 top, 116 all three, 118 top, 134 below, 135 below, 142, 146, 147 top, 152 both, 153, 154 top, 156 both, 160 left and below right, 162 164 below.
The Wimbledon Lawn Tennis Museum page 11 left, 14 left and right, 16 both, 18 right and below, 19 top, 21 both, 23 left and below, 25 right, 29, 30 left, 32, 33 both, 34 top and below, 35 top, 36 top, 37 top, 47, 48 below, 49, 50, 52 below, 53, 54 left, 55 below, 60-61 both, 65 below, 70, 71.